C...

(Twelve Qualities of Christ)

Other books by the same author:

CONSIDER HIM

Hugh B. Black

NEW DAWN BOOKS

GREENOCK, SCOTLAND

© Hugh B. Black 1988

First published 1988 by
NEW DAWN BOOKS
27 Denholm Street, Greenock PA16 8RH, Scotland.

ISBN 1 870944 04 6

Unless otherwise stated biblical references are to the
Revised Version

Cover photo: Craig Richardson

Production and printing in England for
NEW DAWN BOOKS
27 Denholm Street, Greenock PA16 8RH, Scotland
by Nuprint Ltd, Harpenden, Herts AL5 4SE.

Acknowledgements

I am grateful to all those who continue to encourage me to write; to my wife Isobel and daughter Alison for editorial assistance; to Miss Pauline Anderson, Mr Alastair Duff, Miss Jennifer Jack and Mr George Marshall for proof-reading and helpful advice; to Miss Ina Thomson for transcribing the basic text from tape recordings; and to Miss Irene Morrison for her labours in processing the various drafts of the book.

Dedication

To the memory of Amy Carmichael of Dohnavur in whom so many of the qualities of Christ were seen.

Contents

Foreword

It has been a privilege and an inspiration to read and meditate on the qualities of Jesus of Nazareth as discussed in this book. In doing so, the thought came to my mind that this is the greatest man who ever walked this earth— O that all men would take time to study this man's character, and that their greatest ambition in life would be to be like Him, and walk as He walked. We would then have a better world.

These are divine qualities revealed in One Who, although He was the Son of God, was nevertheless human. Because of this, He not only can be touched with the feelings of our weaknesses, but He has the power to deliver us—and best of all—change us into His likeness.

In these days when moral standards are being eroded, and so much tragedy seems to stalk human lives, it is good to turn our eyes upon this man Jesus, and consider Him. This book will help you to do this very thing.

You will find that it is His deep desire to change us into His likeness, and to fill us with His love, His holiness and His power. His earnest prayer was that we should become one with Him, and the Heavenly Father, and with one another, in thought, in word, and deed. We are to behold His glory and be changed by it. Indeed, necessity demands it in order that the world may see and believe that He is the One sent by God—the one and only Saviour.

The author of this study has been a source of inspiration and encouragement to me, my wife and family, and to those we have been in fellowship with over many years. Others have been brought face to face with the subject of these studies, in camp meetings, conferences, and conventions held by Hugh Black, and challenged to a deeper life of holiness and dedication to this wonderful Saviour and Lord—Jesus of Nazareth, the Son of the Living God.

I pray that the Holy Spirit will open your eyes to see Jesus in the pages of this book, and as you behold His glory, you will be changed by that glory into His image.

Bill Kettles
Wellwood
Longforgan
Tayside, Scotland

General Introduction

The first five chapters of this book have been adapted from a series of sermons preached at a summer conference at Wiston (near Biggar in Scotland) in July 1986. Chapter six has been added later to complete the work.

I very much hesitated before proceeding to publish this book. The spoken word and the written word are so very different and I feared that the literary deficiencies of the first chapters might be too great. I allowed myself, however, to be persuaded when it was pointed out that while the style was markedly different from my earlier books it had a certain direct preaching quality in it which might prove acceptable to readers. The very fact that it is different from previous books may also provide variety. I am still, however, very much aware that the material was first presented in sermon and not in essay form. Perhaps you will read with a kindly eye, or should I say ear?

The subject matter needs no introduction. It is lovely to 'consider Him' and meditate on His glorious qualities. I have taken twelve. There are so many more. It may be that you will be encouraged to explore for yourself in this inexhaustible mine. I trust you will find something of value in the nuggets I have found.

Readers of my first book, *Reflections on the Baptism in the Holy Spirit*, commented very favourably on the fact that I had included my testimony, and it was suggested that I should do the same kind of thing in other books. The second book, *Reflections on the Gifts of the Spirit*, contained a good deal of anecdote and at least parts of various testimonies, and in addition had gone to press before I could incorporate the suggestion. The third book, *Reflections on a Song of Love*, was also almost complete and could not be easily altered. It was, however, possible to have testimony in *A Trumpet Call to Women*, and this has also been very favourably received. Accordingly in this book I am including the testimony of Miss Jennifer Jack. This lady found Christ in early years. An only child, she lost both parents as a young woman—her mother having been crippled since Jennifer's birth. The call of God to a deep life came early. Her response to this was full-hearted. As she allowed God to change her, and as she disciplined her own life, He gave her liberally of Himself. Used in the vocal gifts of the Spirit, she is also used in taking people through to the Baptism in the Spirit and in exorcism. Having first worked with Miss Mary Black in leadership of a church in Glasgow, she is now in charge of a church in Falkirk. In her professional capacity she is a teacher in a secondary school. Miss Jack's story makes interesting reading.

PART 1

CONSIDER HIM

(Twelve Qualities of Christ)

1

Peace and Tranquillity

In the morning sessions of our Camp/Conference I quite frequently take themes related to the Baptism in the Holy Spirit; last year I concentrated on gifts of the Spirit, and this year I had wondered whether we should turn our attention to the fruits of the Spirit. For quite a time one of my daughters has been urging me to give teaching on certain practical aspects of Christianity and this seemed a possibility. But what has, in fact, emerged for this series of addresses is, very simply, qualities of Christ. As I pondered the theme I jotted down those that came to mind and took them more or less in the order in which they came. I noticed that they fell into five groups of two, and since there are five morning sessions I thought that that might indeed be very suitable. For this morning the first two are *peace and tranquillity*.

I want you to picture the Lord Jesus Christ. I am sure those of you who have studied literature will realise that different people can read the same book and have differing insights into the characters in it: one perhaps finds a great deal more than do the others—and character appreciation is often affected by experience. Where the study of the qualities of Christ is concerned, you will find that as your spiritual life deepens, as you ponder and meditate, and get to know Christ, your appreciation of His character will also deepen.

Now I want you to turn your mind to two qualities: peace and tranquillity. Of course it is very easy to say right away, Yes, peace—Christ brought peace, He was the Prince of Peace—and it is a lovely thought, the thought of peace and tranquillity; what else is there to say when you have said that? Well, I think there is a very great deal more to say.

When a boy is young, peace is a quality that is peculiarly uninteresting—war, yes; battle, strife, yes, yes, yes; but peace and quietness and tranquillity, please no! But as a boy becomes a man and the man grows older, peace becomes a wonderful quality, even in very natural terms: just peace.

I feel that had we met Christ one of the first things that we would have noticed about Him would have been an aura of peace, a sense of infinite quietness, the peace and the quietness of an extremely deep pool: water unruffled, tranquil, quiet—a feeling of a Person who was complete—a Person in Whom there was no quest, no striving, no restlessness, no agitation.

I have met very few people in my life in whom I felt that there was no longer a quest, that they were totally at home in God, that they were complete—one was the late Principal George Jeffreys, a man who had been very, very deeply used of God. It was as though he had come home. I felt this too as I read of Madame Guyon, that she was complete, and at total peace and rest. She too had come home.

Now there are degrees of peace—there are some of us who may be placid by nature, or have good control of our facial expressions and of our immediate reactions. I personally have always had a great objection to showing anything verging on panic. It is perhaps a natural thing. I remember one young man who on the day on which he bought the engagement ring for his wife-to-be, unfortunately took a wrong train on their way home. He was rather a self-contained young man and quickly realised their mistake but said never a word. The young lady, however, exclaimed so loudly that all in the compartment probably heard. I am sure that young man will have your sympathy!

I remember a recent occasion. We had just bought our present house in Greenock and I was driving home with a visitor one evening after a meeting. We were stopped by the police within about 100 yards of the house. I don't know what they were looking for, or whether I was 'keeping my options open'—a habit of which I am sometimes accused when I occupy two lanes at one time! In any case the police stopped us. 'Sir, what is your car number?' I said, 'I haven't a ghost of a notion.' They went on to ask, 'Where do you live?' and the horrible truth was I didn't know that either—I had just bought the house. I didn't know whether it was 27 or 28—it was just up around the corner anyway. I don't know whether by that time they had recognised who I was, because, as a Headmaster, most of the police knew me, but that ended the episode. By this time my friend, absolutely uptight, exclaimed in incredulous tones, 'And you were as cool as a cucumber!' I didn't think this odd. I didn't reckon there was any reason to be anything but cool—after all it was my car, my house, my business and I wasn't breaking any law. It had nothing to do with the police. My peace was unruffled. Now this kind of peace is often a comparatively light, external thing.

When we come to judge real peace we often see it against a background of trouble. It has a deep down inwardness in it. Christ's soul dwelt in an area where there was perfect tranquillity. He dwelt in God, and God is never hurried. He is never pressurised. There is never a shadow of panic or disturbance in the deeps of God. There

is an eternal calm, an eternal rest. Christ dwelt there.
Christ saw into that deep. He lived in that deep. He was
not particularly taken up with surrounding circumstance,
and this is where we tend to make the mistake. We view
the peripheral, the temporal, the transient; He viewed the
eternal, the permanent, that which was at the heart of
eternity. He was rooted there, and we are so often rooted
down here. Let me illustrate it.

There is a mighty storm, and the boat would appear to
be about to go down. He is asleep in the midst of the ship
and the disciples are petrified. They are filled with fear and
they ultimately waken Him, 'Master, carest Thou not that
we perish?' He arose and rebuked them for their little faith
and with an almost seemingly casual word, as though He
threw it over His shoulder, said, 'Peace, be still!'—and
immediately there was a great calm. The Master of wind
and storm, the Master of sea and sky, the Master of man
was there—'Peace, be still!' That unquiet was not allowed
to enter into Him but the deep quiet that was in Him
moved out and touched the circumstance. A peace that
was not on the periphery—a peace that came from the
heart of eternity.

I want to move now to the hours when the shadow of the
cross is falling athwart His very life. He is about to go
through Gethsemane and Calvary and He knows that the
hour of His agony is very near. With great, great gentleness and kindness He speaks those glorious words, 'In my
Father's house are many mansions; if it were not so, I
would have told you. I go to prepare a place for you. And
if I go and prepare a place for you, I come again, and will
receive you unto myself . . . my peace I give unto you: not
as the world giveth, give I unto you. Let not your heart be
troubled' (Jn 14:2–3, 27).

I want you to see Christ in those lonely hours, for He
was extremely alone—there were none on earth who could
share with Him the experience through which He was

passing. He was exceedingly alone. There was coming a
moment when He would be cut off even from the Father
and hung as a spectacle between Heaven and earth and
those who were nearest to Him would be unable to go with
Him. Into the heart of the garden went Peter and James
and John and they slept there. They could not enter into
the awfulness of Gethsemane, and when He hung on that
cross He was alone in spirit, cut off from all His human
friends. As the shadows began to gather He was intensely
aware of the position. I believe He had an absolute knowledge of what was coming upon Him and He still used
these words—'Let not your heart be troubled'—don't be
upset—don't be torn apart by circumstances—'Ye
believe in God, believe also in Me.' It is as though He
looked at them (and He may have seen consternation—we
don't know) and said, 'Peace I leave with you. My peace I
give unto you. Let not your hearts be troubled.'

Look closely at Christ. The billows are rising all around
Him, and remember He was in the role of the Son of
Man—not in the role of the Son of God. While He never
ceased to be God the Son, by coming into flesh and becoming man, He deliberately emptied Himself and took upon
Himself the form of a servant. He became a man, and by
becoming man accepted certain human limitations. We are
not told how His humanity affected His omniscience—it
may be that He received knowledge from God from stage
to stage as matters unfolded. He was certainly utterly
dependent upon God. He moved by the power of the Holy
Spirit. He wrought His miracles by the power of the
Spirit. In fulfilling the mission He was given, I believe the
word of Satan would be frequently in His ear—'How do
you know you are the Son of God? Are you not deceived?
Why should you have these ideas about yourself?' And as
the shadows darkened I imagine there would be many a
suggestion, 'You are mistaken. Would God have allowed
this if you had been right? Would He have allowed this

cup? Would He have asked you to drink this cup? Is it really God? How can you be quite sure?'—question after question after question—an attempt to break Him and to change His total dependency on God. You can feel the tempest rising, not the storm on the lake, but the storm on the sea of life around Christ, the billows rising—the going of Judas into the night to betray Him, the gathering in the garden, the coming of the soldiers, the taking of Christ, the binding, the carrying away to judgment, to one judgment after another, to the robing with purple robe, the wreathing with crown of thorns, the putting of the mocking staff in His hand, and ultimately the pre-crucifixion lashing which was so severe that men who received it were not expected to recover, the lash cutting to the bone (a lash with metal and leather interwoven), every lash cutting deep, curling around the head, the face, making long the furrows on the back. You can feel the tides rising— Satan's whisper, 'Are you not mistaken? Are you the Son of God? Are you Messiah? Are you not out of the will of God?' And the stakes are driven through His hands and feet. I belive that Satan would be horrifically in pursuit of Christ.

(Recently I have been reading a book about quite a secular matter. Someone who was shot in the hand cried like a child. Evidently it is a fearful experience to be shot in the centre of the hand because of the nerves that meet there. It has a shattering effect upon a person.)

With stakes driven through hands, through feet, the cross is upraised and plunged into the hole prepared with all the rending of flesh. You see Him hanging through these hours in agony and pain and the coming of the sins of the world upon His spotless person, and I think ever the voice of Satan, 'Are you not mistaken? Are you not mistaken? Is it really God that is leading you?' It is in such an hour that you judge the quality of the peace. He can say, 'My soul is exceeding sorrowful even unto death,' but you know and I know, instinctively, that there is no panic in that voice. It is a statement of an agony. There can be a burden that may be almost unbearable but there can be at the same time a peace that is unbreakable and that peace was maintained in His most trying circumstances. Never once do you hear a voice of panic, never once an expression of regret, never a sign of self-centredness or selfishness.

Even in that awful moment when He cried, 'My God, My God, why hast Thou forsaken Me?', we sense depth of anguish but no cringing fear, no voice of hysteria or panic. Under the very shadow of the cross He had instituted the feast of Remembrance. He cared for us. He loved us. His love was outreaching, never self-centred. If you knew that very shortly you were going to be crucified, how deep would your concern be for the salvation of the world? How deep would your concern be for the pain that your body would be about to suffer? Christ thought of others. He lived for others. He moved for others—an unruffled peace from the beginning to the end.

I come now to a part that I particularly want to develop. Elsewhere we read of the peace of God that passes human understanding. We come to the verse I have already quoted—'Peace I leave with you. My peace I give unto you'—and that is the verse for this morning. 'My peace I give unto you.' What ruffles your heart, your spirit, your life? Where are the strains and the stresses coming from— the things that cause an aura of unrest around you? When people come into your presence do they feel peace—do they feel the peace of Christ—or do they feel a nervous reaction—an uptightness, a restlessness? You say, 'But these things are natural.' Of course they are—so is murder. But the naturalness of murder doesn't make it right. 'But I have a nervous disposition.' Of course you have, but God is stronger than your nervous disposition. 'I tend to panic,' you may say. Of course you do, it is natural. Always remember that because a thing is natural it is not necessarily right. Christ changes people. You say, 'I never thought He could change that.' Why in the world did you not think He could change that? For the God who holds the whole world in His Hands, is it a great matter that He should change your disposition? I know quite well as I speak that there are not many of you who really believe that God can change you fundamentally in your natural disposition but I am still telling you that you can be complete in Christ. He did not come to say, 'My peace I give unto one or two of My favourites.' He doesn't know the word 'favourite'. He said, 'My peace I give unto you. Not as the world giveth give I unto you. Let not your heart be troubled.' Do you believe it? Do you believe you can be changed? Those of you who are honest, and that applies to most of you, will no doubt be deeply aware of your inadequacies. I think I am aware of at least some of mine, and on the day that I come to the conclusion that God can't help me in my inadequate areas I will be finished. I believe that you can be totally complete in Christ, and He will take the areas of weakness and pour in His own strength until people who meet you will sense the radiation of the peace of Christ from you, and in a world of turmoil this peace is vital—not the placidity of a half-dead dog but the vibrant life of the peace of God: the feeling that nothing touches you, that nothing troubles you (although those who dwell in the deepest peace carry the heaviest burdens and are most troubled but in a different sense of that word). You can be burdened for the sake of others with prayer burden, spiritual burden, but there is within an eternal quietness, an eternal peace. It is the peace of God.

I close with something that is very relevant. In the field of education over recent years (maybe the last decade or so) there came certain changes. Instead of lessons being approached in an honest straightforward way, things got dressed up in much more psychological language. You had to have aims and objectives. You were not allowed to wander in and teach the honest spontaneous lesson. You had to have defined exactly what you were doing and where you were going and ultimately, according to the behaviourist school at least, it came down to, 'What changes do you want to see in the pupils sitting before you after your lesson?' Well you obviously wanted to see a lot of changes, but apart from the sort of soap and water changes, it was the intellectual changes that you were to be concerned with—the cognitive changes, if you want the jargon. In other words, Roy might be an ignorant boy when he came in but it would be the teacher's objective to have him be less ignorant by the time he went out. To have changes of a cognitive nature accomplished would be the objective of the lesson.

Now, my aim this morning has not been merely to enlighten you intellectually about the qualities of peace and tranquillity, the quietness on the surface of a lake, the inner repose and calmness. You may ponder all these things. You may be interested in these things. You may say, 'That adds up. That makes sense. I understand that, I feel better.' Well, it is no part of my business to have you feel better at the moment (in one sense). In fact it might be much better if you felt worse! What I really am after is not your mere understanding of peace, but a change wrought in you whereby the stress goes, the tension goes, the unquiet goes and the peace of Christ, Christ's own peace, comes into your heart: not that you merely think about change but that you experience it: that something of the glory of that peace catches your imagination and opens your spirit to having it actually come right in and possess your heart. You might not think it a great gift but I tell you if you receive that gift today from the hand of God, the gift of peace, your whole life will change—your whole life will be revolutionised—in that respect you will become like Christ.

If I follow on with other qualities of Christ this week I want you to measure yourself against Him honestly. What kind of a creature are you—jumping around like the proverbial hen on a hot girdle, causing disquiet wherever you go, causing unrest, tension, strain? Do you know we are in a day when the psychologists are frequently conducting courses on stress management? We live in an age of strain; we emanate it, and God is not in it. When He comes there is peace, the Hand of peace touches the life. You say, 'That is true. That is lovely. I like that.' I am not interested at the moment in your liking that. We have all known that. What I am now concerned about is this. Is He going to move out through each one of us in reality—to spread His peace? It is one thing looking at Him and saying it happened through Him. It is another thing to become so Christ-filled that it happens through us.

Now it may be that at the end of this Conference some of you will say, 'I have learned a lot,' and I am giving you fair warning—I am going to say, 'Have you changed a lot?' I am not interested merely in the illumination of your minds but in the obedience of your hearts. I will want to know to what extent you have 'put on the Lord Jesus Christ' and have gone from Camp carrying, radiating and transmitting His presence. So, first warning, measure yourself against Christ. Is the peace that radiated from Him radiating from you? If not, why not, and what are you going to do about it? 'Well,' you say, 'what should I do about it?' Do what Finney would have told you—go on your knees and repent. 'But,' you say, 'It is not a sin.' I say, 'It is a sin—a sin of omission.' 'The fact that I don't have peace?' Yes, a sin—it is a sin—and unless you recognise it as a sin you are never likely to do very much about it. As long as you regard it as a natural disposition that is part of your legitimate way of life you will do not a thing about it, but when you realise that you are giving an unclear reflection of Jesus Christ, that you are letting

Christ down in this world, that you are not a true follower in that you are not showing His characteristics, you will realise that you are in sin and will, I trust, do something about it.

You probably don't like that—do any of us like it? And you will find as we go from quality to quality we will be nailed to the cross until we cry for mercy that we may become in every characteristic like Jesus Christ. It is God's plan that we grow into the maturity of full-grown men and women in Christ, that we radiate Him.

I am aware that I have said little about tranquillity as distinct from peace, perhaps simply because it is not distinct from peace but is rather an aspect of it. Because the two qualities are so interlinked I have concentrated on one.

For me tranquillity is often associated with water. This may be deep and may at times be ruffled. Tranquillity is the quality that seems to come when, after storm, calmness comes over the face of the deep; we often read of tranquil waters. The word speaks of calmness, absence of unrest or bustle. Surely there is that peace, that tranquillity in Christ. Let us aspire to it.

Was it Rees Howells to whom the letter was addressed—something like, 'To the man full of the Holy Spirit, Wales, Britain'? And it reached him. If there came a letter to my town, 'To the person who reminds everybody of Christ, who radiates His peace and tranquillity,' I don't think it would reach me, but I do trust that one day it might reach some of us—known to be just so like Jesus Christ, so full of the Holy Spirit—so full of His peace and tranquillity!

2

Purity and Serenity

This morning I want to go on to the next two qualities that
came to me and take them in the order in which they
came. These are *purity and serenity*. I expect you will
immediately realise that serenity is very much linked with
peace and tranquillity but I want to keep the order in
which the qualities came. I did not plan the order and I
think there is a reason for taking purity before serenity.

I would like you to consider for a moment, especially
those of you who are preachers and teachers and instruc-
tors of others, what your reaction would be were I to say,
'We are going to do things differently this morning. We'll
have a little change. I have given you the theme and I
would like you to come up and preach the sermon on
purity and serenity.' You might suddenly wonder, 'What
can I really say about that—the purity and serenity of
Christ? I think I could maybe speak for about two minutes. We all know Christ was pure but when I've said that,
again what else is there to say? Christ had serenity, yes,
but when I've said that, what else is there to say?' That is
how it might strike you at first but had you time to ponder
a little you might find that instead of the subject being one

to be treated briefly it is in reality profound. I might almost say awesome. Purity is a word that is seldom heard nowadays on the lips of preachers. It is a concept that has too often been put away on a shelf somewhere—as though it was kind of otherworldly—not terribly relevant or real—a bit airy-fairy—something for the imagination— 'purity.'

Now let me tell you that for many years I have been totally convinced that purity and power go hand in hand. People go to God for power, power, power; and they never, or seldom, go to Him for purity. But those who find purity normally find power, and those who find power and fail to allow purity to rule their lives frequently lose their power because the two are inextricably linked, and impurity has a disastrous effect on spiritual life. Any individual who indulges in it to any extent whatever will be affected. Purity is of extreme importance. It is not peripheral. It is not merely a good idea with which God will be pleased. It is absolutely vital and it is exceptionally rarely enjoyed.

I am not speaking in a censorious way. I am human and I know human make-up. I know the problems that face humanity on this front and I think it is proper for us to have a look at these problems.

First, it is part of the natural order of things that there should be reproduction. It is right. It is God-ordained. It is not forbidden, but partly because of the way in which society is organised there can come undue pressures. Young people can have all the instincts for reproduction without a legitimate way of fulfilling natural desire. This pressure can lead to wrong forms of activity. The Bible teaches that marriage is 'honourable in all' and 'the bed is undefiled'; that sexual relations are themselves ordained of God and have nothing in them which is essentially wrong. It's as well to know and recognise this from the beginning. But, in fact, young people grow up nowadays in a society in which there is an extreme distortion of basic things.

From early days pornography is increasingly presented. There are now videos too vile to identify in public meetings. Through television there comes a stream of filth right into our living-rooms. Sewers have opened and perversion is legitimised; our young people grow up very differently now from twenty years ago. You can scarcely open a normal paper, an ordinary national daily paper, without meeting filth left right and centre. Sex is presented in a salacious, polluted way.

What is actually happening is this. Young minds which are very, very vulnerable and very open to deep impressions are having stamped on them that which is unclean from almost their earliest consciousness. I remember in my own case I had an unusual background in that I lived on a farm and we had a great deal of tough labour. In many ways the workers had low standards, to put it mildly. In those early days things were said that to this day I remember—amongst them one or two rhyming couplets which were absolutely filthy. They had a powerful effect on my child mind and what is imprinted in early days has a tremendous potency. It remains because the mind is very vulnerable and takes impressions very deeply.

If you repeated similar couplets to me now at my present age, I wouldn't remember them for an hour but what went in to the mind at that stage—not only of that kind but of other kinds as well—went in very deeply and can be readily recalled. I don't mean that the impurity of these couplets affects me. It doesn't in any way, but I could bring back the memory of the lines in seconds. As a result of exposure to filth young people are becoming desperately polluted at very, very early stages.

When I began to teach I wanted to teach senior classes. I wanted fifth and sixth years as soon as I could get them. I thought I would be able to influence that age group but I soon discovered that nearly all the young people who found Christ came out of first year or the first half of second year. By that time pollution was beginning to set in and it was increasingly difficult to find souls for Christ. I believe that now the defilement, frequently quite deep, takes place very much earlier, in primary, never mind in secondary schools. You can see the uncleanness in faces. You can see the sexual troubles that have begun even at these very early ages and a fearful fight can ensue for a young life which is also wanting to find Christ. Sexual defilement frequently prevents a soul finding Christ and affects growth in Christ. Never deceive yourself about this. You cannot be impure and holy; these cannot go together. The natural part of you will opt for impurity and that cannot live with holiness. There is no point in your trying to find a place of compromise. God will have cleanness in the inner parts, an absolute cleanness.

I have noticed another thing: when society moves strongly in a wrong direction things that are quite objectionable at the beginning of the movement quickly become tolerated. Let me give you an example. There was a play by Shaw which was broadcast many years ago and which, I understand, had one swear word in it. The broadcast almost caused a national crisis. I don't remember what the word was exactly, but it was a very mild word by the standards of the 'eighties and the outcry and the furore over the public use of that word was tremendous. Nowadays it wouldn't raise an eyebrow. It takes a great deal now to shock the public. Indeed a fearful amount which comes across doesn't seem to shock at all. Gradually defences are weakened and resistance drops. 'Well, it's happening. It's happening everywhere. Why make a fuss?' You find that your own standards are affected. What would have shocked you rigid twenty years ago is accepted as part of life. I am not saying you indulge in these things or condone them but your standards are affected. The fact that an old lady is mugged and raped is still quite shocking. At one time it would have horrified you for months, for years.

Now it doesn't have time to do that because you open the newspaper next morning and you find something equally vile and horrible and you move from one horror to another. A resistance builds up and until these things come very close to your own person or your family or somebody you know, you are scarcely affected. It is as though the flood of sin and darkness and filth has become so great that it has overflowed and been accepted.

There is another area in which the change has been very marked. I remember my university days. Students never were models of perfection but in those days boys and girls didn't live together to any great extent. You might have an isolated pair here and there but, if so, they were the talk of the campus, whereas now the incidence of students sharing accommodation and cohabiting is actually quite horrendous. That no longer shocks me because I've become accustomed to it, although I am still shocked at the fact that Christian students quietly accept this as a way of life. I am not saying that they themselves participate in it, but the fact of people living together before marriage has become for many of the young generation an accepted pattern. Frequently those involved are not even ashamed of it. They are not embarrassed when it is discovered. If you don't discover it yourself, they'll tell you quite openly, 'There is nothing hidden about it. This is just how we've chosen to live.' [A mature student reading this script commented, 'I think many of them haven't the faintest idea that it might be wrong.']

I remember a case of two young unmarried teachers who were living together quite openly in a district from which pupils were drawn for the school in which they taught. In my own early days in teaching this would never have been tolerated. The change that has come is a radical change and one of the dangers is that we accept the change and no longer allow it to shock us. The standards come tumbling down, and subconsciously we feel, 'Well, God will be pleased if people don't do that—if they refrain from living together before they are married; if they refrain from sexual intercourse before marriage or outside of marriage.' Let me tell you it takes a great deal more than that to please God. You can be innocent on both of these counts and still be deeply polluted and deeply displeasing to God. Refraining from these things is not God's standard of holiness or God's standard of purity. You can refrain from such things and still be polluted in His eyes. Many, many of the people that I have to deal with in exorcism for uncleanness may have refrained from both of these things and yet demons of lust and uncleanness have taken possession of their bodies.

You ask, 'What do you mean? What do you mean?' I mean Christ has a standard. You think you haven't committed adultery—that's fine. 'Behold I say unto you that He that looketh on a woman to lust after her hath committed adultery with her already in his heart.' Christ isn't surveying the periphery of your life and judging that if you haven't been guilty of adultery you have done well. He isn't looking at the outward things. He is looking into the heart, down into the centre of your being and He sees if, from that centre, there rise unclean thoughts, unclean desires, unclean imaginations. He knows if your spirit is feeding in the imaginative realm on that which is polluted and soiled. You don't do this or that because you know that to do so would be wrong or you might be found out, but there's no reason, you may tell yourself, for not thinking about these things, for not day-dreaming about them and enjoying the day-dreaming, living in a polluted realm, reading polluted literature, watching polluted programmes. Filth gets into the spirit amazingly quickly, amazingly easily and amazingly potently. I know what I'm talking about in this realm. People can come to me for deliverance and when I examine the situation I may find that nothing more than a thought from a book caused the entities to get in. You say, 'Is that true? Do you mean the people didn't do anything other than that? No, that's all they needed to do. They only had to indulge in unclean thoughts. There may have been a background. It seems that a comparatively small thing can open a weak area in the personality and they are caught. I don't mean that every unclean thought that passes through a person's mind brings in a demon. It doesn't, but there are times when a demon can gain entrance in as seemingly small a way as that. I have known of a person living a very, very clean life and suddenly for the first time, in adult years, coming on a pornographic piece of literature and thinking, 'I wonder what it's like after all . . .' and reading, and being polluted and, I think in that case, being tormented for years before being set free. Christ's standard of purity and man's are remarkably different. If you want to reach the high heights with God you will become pure. You will put the unclean out. You will replace the unclean thought with the clean thought. You will turn immediately to Christ and in His Presence you will find no impurity—it can't live in His Presence. Quite frequently, in exorcism a person has to retrace the steps by which the entity got in and I have known me say, 'Remember what you did. Picture Christ watching it.' I feel a writhing under my hand, like a serpent writhing. Demons can't stand that. Just picture Christ seeing all, hearing all, knowing all, and in that pure Presence the demon power is in an agony, an absolute agony. Impurity and Christ never go hand in hand.

I don't consider this a matter on which I can say, 'Well, I've preached this and they all understand it now and all is well.' It's sticky. It takes discipline. It takes a way of life. It takes an attitude, and I don't believe you will ever get over it by merely looking at it and fighting with it. As you look at it and fight with it, you can get to a stage where you may even enjoy that, because you feel it gives you a legitimate right to think about it. It's a most sticky thing to deal with. Do you know that even in exorcism I have come on a case where the person concerned warned me part-way through the exorcism that the very concentration on that area was raising difficulties, and there was in them a desperate desire to plunge back into the filth, into the sin that had caused the condition. I didn't know what to do. It seemed that to go on praying might make things worse and my hand was still on the person's shoulder. I really didn't know what to do. I waited for a moment and then a very, very lovely thing happened. I don't know that this ever happened to me before or since in just the same way. I suddenly sensed Christ Himself come in a very particular way. There was a leap of joy within me and I spoke aloud: 'I have no more to do with this case. Christ has come. Christ is in charge. Christ is come against the demon power.' And I stepped back. It was lovely. It was as if I had nothing else to do. Oh, that demon was absolutely petrified, absolutely—no more insolence, no more anything. Out it went, and speedily. It could not stand the burning, immediate Presence of Christ. There was no more talk from the tormented person about going back to the filth hole. Christ brings with Him absolute purity.

Now I fear I may not greatly help you by merely getting you to think about this kind of thing and repent of it to the best of your ability. And I want you to know that masses of people are affected by uncleanness to some degree, at least in thought. It's not a one or two business, this. Uncleanness is endemic, and I mean that. It affects nearly everybody to a greater or lesser extent and Satan has people thinking they are alone in this particular mess, that they are different. Not so. A wide, wide range of Christians are affected and, as I have said, I don't think I can help you by merely getting you to recognise this and repent of it. I might get you to both of these stages and leave you little better and even possibly with a greater feeling of guilt on your conscience.

You say, then, 'What are you going to do about it and why are you talking to us about this if things are as bad as that?' I really know of only one way out of this. You do need to recognise the position. You do need to repent of it. You do need to have a right attitude and if, deep down, you don't have a right attitude you need at least to be willing to be made willing to have a right attitude. At that point God can step in and produce the miracle. I have often found that where there is no vision the people perish. When the moment comes that you realise that if you continue to go down the wrong road you will never attain your goal, or your crown, or accomplish your mission—there is hope. If you deal with your sin or rather allow God to deal with it, you will be set free to become an overcomer and fully fulfil the call of God. You get the vision in your mind, the glory in your mind, the far call, the eternal horizon, and for love of Him, for the fulfilment of your destiny you are not prepared to allow any sin or any kind of impurity to prevent that happening. Like an athlete who is prepared to cut out many types of food to attain the crown, so the runners in this race for God cut out the defilement that they may attain the purity of God and become overcomers in Him. And if you cannot be stimulated to fulfilment of that high ambition you are likely to have a very difficult time with various areas of pollution. There are so many who prefer to settle for the seeming joy of the moment which is really no joy and which is transient. As you bite the forbidden fruit, it turns to ashes in your mouth. Are you powerless? Then very possibly you are also impure. Are you pure? Then almost certainly in some areas at least you are powerful. Power and purity are for ever linked—weakness and impurity walk hand in hand. There is a way in Christ of total deliverance—there is total freedom in Jesus, the Son of God.

You say, why did you include serenity? Because with purity goes serenity. It is a wonderful word, serenity.

Serene—you picture someone who has been through the battle, through the tempestuous waters, who knows the ups and downs, and there is a look that suggests that nothing in this world is going to shake him. 'Hope, serene as a star.' Serene—unchanging, bright, shining, glorious—the purity of Christ, the serenity of Christ.

He came walking into the villages of men, serenity on His brow, calmness, peace and tranquillity. So gentle, so lovely, so kind and as He came, the demons writhed and shook. They trembled and as He drew nearer they could not stand that Holy Presence. They screamed out, 'We know Thee, who Thou art, Thou Holy One of God. Art Thou come to torment us before our time?' So potent, so powerful, so pure. Do you realise that that purity spelt hell to the demon powers? Do you realise that that holiness was a burning, raging fire to their spirits? Jesus Christ the Son of God. And He calls you to be like that.

I have told you that the point of these homilies is to produce change in you and me. I want to encourage you to be ambitious for the purity and serenity of Christ, to aspire to the absolute standard of Christ—that there be no unclean desire, thought, imagination—that when the pool of your life is thoroughly searched by the eyes of God He may see clear water right to the very bottom and no impurity at all. Purity is a positive quality. There is a force of life, a drive, a power, in purity. It is a living thing. He would transmit it to you that people whom you meet may feel it and be affected. The demons will cringe before it for they will feel it too. When you are impure your spirit is bound. It is earth-bound or hell-bound. When you are free with the freedom of God your spirit soars. The horizons are infinite. You know true freedom—the freedom of God.

Do I despise impure people? I don't. I have tremendous compassion for people caught in impurity, in the chains of it, in the binding power of it, in the strength of the lust of it. I don't look down on people who are caught in that trap. I have the anger of God against it, but the compassion of Christ for the person who is suffering in it. Don't let the wicked one so deeply discourage you that you can't get up and fight. Begin now—be prepared to be changed, until you are as pure as the Son of God. 'What,' you say, 'as pure as the Son of God?' Yes, I mean that—that is the purity He wants in us—His own purity; and we can feel the joy and the rippling happiness and the glory of that purity even as we think about it.

3

Strength and Courage

The qualities I have taken are peace and tranquillity, purity and serenity. I know the sermon on purity and serenity has had quite a profound effect. There are people who really do want to reach the heights with God and the question of purity is one that faces most of humanity to some degree or other. The theme before us this morning is rather different. It is *strength and courage*.

I want you to consider these qualities as they were revealed in the life of Christ. That is a wise and interesting thing to do, but again there isn't really a lot of point in doing it if the matter is merely to be left there. I want you now to look at these qualities or the lack of them in your own life. Again, I want you to realise that God is minded to change people— that we can be changed into His likeness—that we may have his attributes—that we may become like Him—that we may have His peace, his tranquillity, His purity, His serenity, His strength, His courage.

Shall we look first at strength? I indicated on an earlier occasion that the quality of peace was not one that boys particularly consider as of great importance; similarly tranquillity and serenity are not things that are high on their list of priorities or about which they dream. They dream rather of courage and strength, of bravery and heroism, of war and conflict. Often when they are thinking in terms of strength they are thinking of the Samsons or Goliaths of this world, or of Atlas who carried the world on his shoulders. When I was a boy, H. Broom was the mighty man. His were the developed muscles, and I read that I too might have a body like his. I promptly bought the muscle developing gear and set to work! Boys had their own idea of strength. It meant great in proportion, muscular and so on. With maturity there comes the realisation that people can have all these attributes but be, in fact, very weak people: that physical strength is not always, or necessarily, allied with other types of strength. The emphasis on the physical declines. Indeed I suppose the importance of physical strength to society generally, began to pass with the invention of potent means of destruction such as gunpowder—a bullet killed a great strong man just as easily as it killed a weaker man. (It doesn't really show any particular preference although it is probably easier to hit a big man!) Physical strength is not particularly important in modern times.

I wonder what your definition of real strength is. Ponder it for a moment. How do you judge strength? What kind of man is a strong man? You may say, 'I think he is the kind of man who has a craggy jaw. He never gives in. He digs his heels in and refuses to budge, etc. etc.' Actually you are probably giving a good description of a stubborn mule and stubbornness is not necessarily strength. You will sometimes find that a stubborn person is refusing to act sensibly and his seeming strength is, in fact, really weakness. A wonderful animal is the mule, and some of us share its qualities to a greater or lesser extent. You try to pull it and it won't come. You try to push it and it won't go. I have amongst my acquaintances one who is peculiarly mulish at times and I have indicated to her that the only way to deal with the mule is to light a fire under its tummy. That does produce a reaction. It really does move if you do that. Well, there are some of us who need something like that to happen to propel us into action. If you've got a mulish tendency in you, recognise it as such because it is not a strength; it is, in fact, a real source of weakness.

So what is strength? There are some qualities that are perhaps best understood by an illustration and by considering the quality in action. I want you to think of a person under pressure. Think of Christ under pressure and of how He reacted. He came under pressure almost immediately after He started, or was about to start, His public ministry. He came under pressure from Satan in the temptations in the wilderness. Perhaps I should say Satan tried to apply pressure: 'Do this. Make the stones bread. Throw yourself down from the temple. Get the kingdoms of this world to be yours by bowing down and worshipping me. You listen to me'—the pressure of the satanic voice.

Many of us are too glib about Satan and we don't treat him with the carefulness that we should. Christ heard but gave no consideration to what Satan said. He didn't allow the suggestions of Satan to get into His mind. He recognised the voice that spoke and He uttered the word of God, 'Man shall not live by bread alone . . . . Thou shalt not tempt the Lord thy God . . . . Thou shalt worship the Lord thy God and Him only shalt thou serve . . . .' His mind was filled with the voice of God and He had no room within Him for the voice of Satan. This is something that it's very wise to learn right from the beginning. Don't argue with Satan. Don't consider the satanic suggestion. Most of us get caught by giving consideration to the suggestions that Satan makes. The wise thing is to refuse to consider them at all, to banish them totally, to ignore them. This is a very difficult thing to do but it is very fruitful and leads to great blessing and victory. This I believe is what Christ did. The devil, on the other hand, would have had Him think: 'That's not a bad idea. I am hungry. I've been fasting for forty days and the fast is over and I could make these stones bread. Why shouldn't I? What's wrong with it anyway? There is a tradition that the Messiah will come down from the temple and if I did that the whole of Israel would know overnight that the Messiah had come. It does seem so reasonable. After all, I did come into the world that the kingdoms of the world should become the kingdoms of God and His Christ. What is wrong with the idea? It seems very plausible.'

Christ knew that the source of any such ideas was satanic. It was not Divine; and I don't believe he ever really considered any one of them for one moment. Instead He pronounced the word of God. The Spirit, I believe, would bring forcibly to His mind the word, the truth, the right action, and the pressure of Satan had no power over Him.

In a very short time He was to find Himself at the wedding in Cana of Galilee and meet a different kind of pressure. People were really getting—in our jargon— 'uptight'. They had run out of wine, which was a great embarrassment to the master of the feast and no doubt to the bridal couple as well, and if it was the bride's mother who supplied the food and drink in those days, I imagine she would be even more agitated than some of you mothers are wont to be in our day—really agitated—no wine! Even Mary, Christ's mother, had become concerned. I think Mary was an exceptionally lovely person. I always have done. It's a great shame that because of her veneration in Catholic circles, Protestants have often swung in an opposite direction and treated her as though she was a person of little account. I don't think so at all. I think she was a very exceptional person, a wonderful person, gentle and sweet and gracious and the kind of person who would feel for others. Are there people embarrassed at the wedding? Are there people in difficulty here? I think she would care. I think she was sensitive and would pick up the vibrations. She would pick up the feeling. In her concern she goes and puts pressure on Christ. 'They've got no wine.' And what does He say?—'Woman, what have I to do with you? Mine hour is not yet come.' Now that's not the harsh way in which we use the word 'woman'.[1] In our day the word has a roughness in it. I think the position could be paraphrased as follows: 'Lady, what have I to do with you? Mine hour has not yet come. Mary, you have your role. You have your place. You are My mother and you have My respect and My love but you know there is one place in which you must never interfere. You must never come between God and Me. I will know when My hour is come. The Holy Spirit is within Me. Do not push Me. Do not try to influence Me. I am under the orders of Another.' Would that the world generally knew that about Christ and Mary. 'Who is my mother? Who are my brethren? They that do the will of God.' Christ resists both human and satanic pressure. He allows neither Satan nor those nearest and dearest to Him to direct His course. Towards the end Peter tried again. 'Not so, Lord. You say you are going to die in Jerusalem—not so, not so.' 'Get thee behind me, Satan. Thou savourest the things of man and not the things of God.' He totally refused pressures of friends or enemies or demons. This is strength. Single-eyedness, single-mindedness—dependence wholly, solely and completely on the Divine.

Now, what about you? What about me? 'You know I really think you ought to do such and such. I have been pondering this and I am quite sure you have made a mistake here, there and yonder, and that you ought to . . .' and you say, 'Right enough. There is something in that.' And then somebody else catches you and gives you another story and you say, 'There's something in that too. Maybe I should change course.'

I used to know a headmaster (that is, in the days before headmasters became perfect!)—he was a kind man but a very weak man and his staff were quite convinced that to nobble him effectively you only needed to be the last to see him. One would go in and there he would be sitting recovering perchance from a hangover from the night before. You put your case and, 'Ah, that's a good idea. Yes, you go ahead.' And, of course, it disrupted half the school and put half the staff into a ferment. Another would storm in to see him. Things were then reversed and so it went on. You had to time your entry wisely to gain your ends. If you were last in you were all right. Things would go your way—at least temporarily.

I liked that old man but oh, he did cause trouble! He used to come into a classroom where law and order prevailed and have a bright notion. 'I know what you are thinking about, you wee rascals. I mind when I was a boy . . .' and he would tell a class of wicked doings of his youth that would never have entered their heads. Pandemonium by the time he went out! That headmaster was a character! He had a great sense of humour but he was weak. He could be pushed this way and that. Basically he was not a strong man.

How do you react under pressure? Are you pig-headed, and is the very fact that somebody is telling you to do something almost enough to cause you to refuse? Do you mistake that for strength? Or are you blown around like a weather vane with every wind that blows? That too is weakness. Or do you live with two ears?—you'll know what I mean in a moment—with a natural ear that is open and understands what is being said, but with another ear, a spiritual ear that is open to God alone, and is largely uninfluenced by what the first ear hears, unless what it hears coincides with what God is saying, and no matter how strong the pressures around you may be (and sometimes they are very, very strong), do you have that clarity and integrity and determination that God's voice alone will be obeyed? 'Oh,' you say, 'I think I can understand that—

that's not too difficult.' Actually it can be extremely difficult. There are quite a number of us who don't really have very much difficulty if we find that we are being opposed. It is almost natural for us to say, 'No.' That I find is not the most difficult thing to handle, but there are some of us who have recently been involved in a particular case where in sheer human consideration and compassion for an individual, we have maybe sometimes been a little deaf to the voice of God and a little too open to a voice of pleading. It can be very difficult when there is a piteous note in the voice and a plea for help, of a kind which God is forbidding, to act on God's terms, and not on our own terms. It is sometimes very difficult to resist that kind of pressure totally and listen only to the voice of God. You find in the end you've got to come to that point and pain has sometimes got to be inflicted. Sometimes one of our first duties is to inflict pain. That's something that many people do not easily understand but it is true. It can happen where a person has to be cut off from a fellowship. When certain types of difficulties arise you sometimes have to be extremely tough and firm. Character is often revealed in the face of pressure.

There is a second area I would like to consider for a moment—strength in the face of praise. There are many people who can withstand a great deal but they are not proof against praise. It goes to their heads immediately. A little touch of flattery, a little deference, a little adulation and you find that they are not as strong as you thought— they can be undermined that way. Where they may be strong under certain types of pressure they may be very weak in the face of praise.

Have you ever looked closely at the life of Christ? He wrought wonderful miracles. Often in one day miracle followed miracle, and the crowds could jostle to make Him a king—and what did He do? At eventide did He gather His disciples and say: 'That was a wonderful day. We really did well today. It was glorious. Tell me how you felt. Tell me how you reacted. Tell me what the crowds are saying'? Never, never, never! He withdrew into desert places. He went up to the mountain top to be alone with God. His strength was impervious to praise. He sought no adulation from men.

Now I don't mean that there isn't a time to praise. Sometimes a person is in much need of encouragement and a word, not of praise for the person, but a recognition of the action of God through the person, can be a great encouragement and I advise you not to be stinting with that. Be careful, however, not to feed the ego or the vanity of the person concerned.

Instinctively one knows that Christ would never stumble through the praise of any human being. What about blame? Strength in the face of pressure, praise, blame.

That is maybe the one some of you feel you are most familiar with. You are blamed. Aren't we all to a greater or lesser extent? You've got to be very careful about blame because in some cases we richly deserve it. We must be careful to consider the criticisms objectively and honestly and accept blame where it is deserved. That is not, however, the kind of blame I am speaking of. It is unjustified blame I have in mind. We have acted for God in all honesty and are blamed, and not only are we blamed but there is a strong attempt to have us change our course.

There is a situation which is, in fact, very recent, and upon some of our people came fearful pressure to alter course. They were much blamed for the course they were taking and one of them in particular was deeply disturbed. It had a shattering effect, more than she could easily stand. You will find that if you launch out in spiritual warfare there will come times when you are under extreme censure and you can react to this in various ways. Some get quite upset and instead of realising and being thankful that they are in God's training school, they allow resentment to come in. All right, your nature is such that you find this difficult. Then this provides opportunity for your improvement. This provides opportunity for you to become strong in that area, not to run away from it or become discouraged but to let God strengthen. Consider God as a perfect trainer. A young man goes into the hands of an athletics coach or a boxing trainer. He shows his paces and comes in from the first run or the first ten rounds in the ring. Now the trainer doesn't seem to be the slightest bit interested in what he has done well, the good points of the performance. He says scarcely a word about them, but he does have a lot to say about the areas of weakness! He then provides a programme that is going to probe these areas of weakness. He devises exercises that are going to make the young man smart, whether he be a runner or a boxer. The very things the man is worst at, the very muscles that are weakest are the ones that are now being dealt with. Pressure comes to produce change.

Now when you and I come into the Hands of God, God brings pressure on the weak areas and He allows us to come into circumstances which expose those weaknesses so that we may change, that we may grow, that we may develop, that we may become strong. And it is the will of God that we become strong in the way that Christ was strong: then we do not break.

In attempting to draw all of this together I am reminded of an insight I once had on man's breaking point. Sometimes, in earlier days, you might see a ship in harbour being held by great ropes. You might think, 'Oh, these are strong ropes. They must take a tremendous strain.' Now no matter how thick any rope ever is, let enough pressure be applied and the rope will snap. It has a breaking point. Iron chains too have breaking points, steel cables break and there is no man born who does not have a breaking point. All that needs to happen is to have enough pressure applied. Peter was particularly strong and he did not break

nearly as easily as most people would have done, but he
did have a breaking point about which he was ignorant
when he vowed eternal loyalty to Christ. But one day he
realised most painfully that this, in fact, was the case, and
that in some ways was perhaps the beginning of wisdom
for Peter; for when a man realises this he no longer
depends on his own strength; he knows that he will break
when the pressure gets too great. There is hope then that
he may begin to look to God.

Don't say, 'I wouldn't have a breaking point.' You don't
know what it might be like under the influence of mind-
bending drugs. You don't know what it might be like in a
hundred and one circumstances, but I do know this, that
Peter ultimately found a new plane of living. He no longer
depended on his own strength; he depended on the Divine
and he would find that in Christ there is no breaking point
at all. There is a total and an eternal strength when we
learn the secret of the exchanged life, and enter into this
dimension.

So, if I could sum up, Christ was centred on God. He
was not vulnerable to human pressure, satanic pressure,
human praise, human blame. These were all external,
peripheral things of no real moment. There was something, or rather Someone, Who was basic in His life and
that was God and the will and way of God. He was tuned
in that direction. He was linked to God and being linked
He was drawing infinite strength, unbreakable strength
from Him. You see the agony of Gethsemane, the judgments, the crown of thorns, the mocking robe, the lash-
ings, the cruelty of the crucifixion and yet you know that
serenity is for ever on that brow. Is He screaming in panic?
Never. He turns to the dying thief: 'Today shalt thou be
with me in Paradise.' He is thinking of another from the
midst of an intolerable agony. His was a strength that is
eternal, a strength that is Divine.

Remember what I have said—the point of my teaching
is that you be changed, that I be changed—not that we

stand and admire that infinite strength of Christ but that we partake of it; that we so allow ourselves to be moved on by the Holy Spirit that we become strong with the strength of God—immovable, rock-like, yet totally flexible in His hand.

Strength and courage. You have found that the second quality I have taken on each occasion until now is more briefly treated than the first. Sometimes the first shines a light on the second, like peace and tranquillity, purity and serenity, in so far as they are linked. Strength and courage also spring from the same root. Did you ever notice that Christ never shows one slightest touch of fear? And I daren't even mention the word 'cowardice' in the same breath as His Name. When they sought to take His life at an early stage He passed through their midst unscathed and went right on with His work. He did not turn aside for a moment. When his enemies came to arrest Him in the garden of Gethsemane I believe He was the calmest person in the whole company. Peter struck the high priest's servant. I think he meant to kill him but partly missed and cut off his ear instead. Christ put the ear back on and healed the servant. I believe there was an outflashing of Divine glory when the arresting band fell back as dead. Ultimately Christ allowed Himself to be taken—no panic, no cowardice, no fear. You see Him standing in that hall when Peter betrayed him with oaths and curses. Christ looked at him—you feel the penetration but also the serenity of that look. Taken from judgment to judgment; standing there before Pilate, 'Thou wouldest have had no power against me except it were given thee from above; therefore he that delivered me unto thee hath greater sin.' Jesus was the true judge. Jesus was in control. Jesus was unperturbed.

Having instituted the Communion Feast just a short time before, under the very shadow of the cross, His thought was totally for others, for you and for me in a later generation. Unruffled, totally courageous, to Judas He said, 'That thou doest do quickly,' and Judas, driven by the Prince of Darkness, as one has said, 'went out into the darkness to do a dark deed.' Christ went out into Gethsemane and there wrestled at the very borders of life and death, anguish forcing drops like blood falling down to the ground. Christ in agony. He prayed fervently and He came to the very height of the crisis. Adam had faced a choice one day and he said by action, 'Not Thy will but mine be done.' Christ reversed it: 'Not My will but Thine be done,' and He took the cup. It was as if the human Jesus said, 'The cup is bitter but if it cannot pass I will drink it' and He drank it to the last bitter drop. He turned not aside. With total courage, He faced His judges. To Herod He made no plea for His life. God had spoken to Herod through John the Baptist. Herod had beheaded John. I believe God had nothing more to say to Herod, nor ever will have, until the eternal judgment, but for a long time Herod had wanted to see Jesus. He now found that Jesus did not speak one word to him. When God has nothing to say to a man, neither has Jesus. Let me also say this—when God has nothing to say to a man, neither should you. (That word is to those of you who run after people whom God has cut off. This sometimes happens, perhaps not often, but occasionally it does. I don't want you to interpret this wrongly because there are many, many people in difficulty over their faith who should be comforted and helped. There is a time and place to run after people for Christ's sake and their own.)

Follow right to the cross, right to the intolerable anguish of Calvary—never a plea for mercy, but, 'He, when He was reviled, reviled not again.' Never a curse, but, 'Father, forgive them; for they know not what they do.'

Don't you love Christ? Don't you admire Him tremendously? Glorious in His strength, glorious in His courage, a total bravery. It has encouraged many another in later generations to go through martyrdom. You may say, how is it possible? How is it possible to endure martyrdom considering the weakness of the flesh—how endure pain to the depth that can be inflicted on the human body?

First let me say it's not as wise for those to boast who are putting their armour on as it might be for those who are taking it off, and there are stories that reach us from behind the Iron Curtain and elsewhere of incredible bravery and courage. There are stories that reach us of people who break in the torture chambers and it is not wise to be too sure as to what we might do in similar circumstances, but I do know from one comparatively small personal experience that God's strength is available to His servants in time of need.

In my early days I was in dispute with the police over open-air work. I won't go into all the detail of it but hundreds of people used to gather regularly and many were converted. The police got very agitated at times and tried to force me to move from the site when they had no authority to do this. To cut a long story short, there came a genuine misunderstanding on one occasion where they had had a complaint and came to deal with it and I thought they had come to break up the meeting. I told the person concerned to stay where he was and as a result they arrested me and took me to jail. I was physically assaulted in the Police Office and in the cell, and there came a moment just as the violence started where I had a choice—to go into God, or to resist at a human level. Fortunately I chose to go into God, and it was a most remarkable experience. It was as if I went out of the body and watched what was happening as I was being struck and left ultimately lying on the cell floor. I had no pain. It must have been an extremely frustrating experience to those who did the beating. In fact there were parts of my body that had been hit and I didn't know about it until certain feelings began to come into them a day or two later. I was taken into a realm where I was totally immune from pain. (In later days as a head teacher relations with the police became very good indeed. The officer mainly concerned in this incident later apologised.)

That was a very small matter, comparatively speaking, but I suddenly realised I understood the martyrs as I had never understood them before. God could come like that. I understood Blandina, who had been ripped by a wild cow in the Roman arena. When they dragged her out and revived her they found she was in ecstasy not in agony. I suddenly realised that there can be a living in the Divine dimension that makes you strong—it makes you courageous with a strength and courage that are not your own. These things are not natural but are Heavenly and Divine.

Again, I reiterate that the point of this teaching is to produce change; to take your human weakness and have it changed to Divine strength. To have your cowardice in so far as you suffer from it (and we all do more or less, I suppose) and have it changed to Divine courage. To be like Christ. Let me keep this before you. The point is to be like Christ—to let Christ live His life through us in power and glory: His life through us—peace, tranquillity, purity, serenity, strength and courage.

Does He appeal to you? He certainly appeals to me— wonderfully!

Notes

[1] In his *Life of Christ*, Dean Farrar comments that 'the address "Woman" was so respectful that it might be, and was, addressed to the queenliest, as by the Emperor Augustus to Cleopatra and not infrequently to princesses in Greek tragedy, [and] so gentle that it might be, and was, addressed at the tenderest moments to the most fondly loved (Jn 20:15; 19:26).

'And "what have I to do with thee?" is a literal version of a common Aramaic phrase which, while it sets aside a suggestion and waives all further discussion of it, is yet perfectly consistent with the most delicate courtesy and the most feeling consideration.'

4

Love and Compassion

The next qualities for our consideration are *love and compassion*.

Now love is a strange word. It has, in fact, quite a number of meanings. You may read of 'the four loves' in C.S. Lewis. You may study the subject in an academic way if you will, but I want to keep things very simple and very clear-cut in this study. I want to focus our attention immediately and directly on the Lord Jesus Christ Himself and the quality of love revealed in and by Him.

Have you noticed that there is no sentimentality in Christ at all? You never get a feeling of 'sentimental' love—and I'm putting inverted commas round 'sentimental' because there is sentiment which is commendable—but the way in which the word sentimental is often used does not apply to Christ. In His love there is never any affectation or pretence of affection. There is nothing that appeals to, or feeds, the flesh. There is no pandering to or providing for the flesh. His love is an austere, wonderful, glorious love. It is a real force. It is potent. It never dies. It goes to a cross and lives for ever. In our western society with our traditions and customs we suffer greatly from wrong notions of love. Not only society in general but the Church itself suffers badly from similar notions and this can lead to very unfortunate consequences.

There are people who come into our fellowship and almost immediately remark on the wonderful sense of the love of God that they feel. They are at home and they settle in deeply. There are others who come in and fail to settle and after a time exclaim, 'There is no love in this place!' They haven't been hugged and fêted and they think we are a cold lot of Scots. The people didn't embrace them when they came in (as though an embrace is an ultimate expression of love). They didn't put out the red carpet—didn't invite them into a light social group and pander to their pride and vanity. 'There is no love in this place. They don't make much of me in this place, don't put me on a pedestal in this place. They treat me as an ordinary person and I'm not!'

What is love? Christ cared almost infinitely for people. I don't want to spend time on peripheral things today. I want to come down to a very deep level and I want to come down to it very quickly.

I think we become terribly confused about likes and dislikes, love and lack of love, because we don't appreciate a very basic distinction. Christ's love for you is not based on what you are, whereas most people's love for others is based on what others are. Let me give you an example. You meet someone and you like him. You get to know him and you begin to find that he behaves unkindly. He is critical of you when you are not present. He is quite capable of making a joke at your expense and your liking begins to run out the way water goes through a sieve. He is not really the fine person you thought him to be. In fact he is not a nice person at all and not only do you not love him, you now positively dislike him because of what he does and because of what he is.

There's almost a humorous side to this. You find that there are perhaps two who come together, either of the same sex or of different sexes. It's not necessarily romantic love but oh, it's just wonderful. The two get to know each other a little better and one finds that the other is not quite so wonderful. 'Oh, she is still a very fine person but you know I was surprised about this and I was rather disappointed in that, and she is not really just all that I thought she was at the beginning.' Give it time . . . give it time.

Those of you who have read *Stalky & Co.* will remember the story of the dead cat. It was strategically placed above King's dormitory. Prout's boys were having revenge and one said of the recently deceased pussy, 'Just give it time. It's just a gentle whiff now but give it time.' Sure enough, a few more days passed and it became an absolute pollution! King was digging up the drains to see where the smell was coming from. 'Just give it time' . . . and just you give people time. As they get to know each other better do they get closer? Oh no, it doesn't always work that way. The more people get to know each other the less close do they frequently become. They know each other better. 'This,' you may say, 'is terrible.' But is it not frequently true?

Let's get to the bottom of this right away. There is nothing in us that wears. Nothing of fallen nature that has eternity in it. Nothing. You say, 'I've got some nice qualities.' That's what you think. In my view in corrupt nature there is nothing that is infinitely attractive. We are terribly human and at the roots we are terribly not nice. Human nature is not nice. It is human nature in itself I am speaking of. After you have known a person for a time you often say, 'That's it. I've got to the bottom of that pool, I know all there is to know about him and it's not satisfying.'

People are very loth to come to this point or to acknowledge it. This really means death to self-esteem. This is death to human self. This is death to carnality. People don't like it. We all like to think there are some nice things

about us. Many people are slow to recognise the poverty
and inadequacies that lie deep down in the human heart.
You think there are some nice things there. Well, rightly
or wrongly, I have come to the conclusion that human
nature in itself, in its indisciplined state, is not nice. It is
selfish and it is self-centred. It has a price. But Christ
changes human nature. Christ changes people, and when
you meet His life in another, when you meet transformed
personality in another, you meet that which is lovely, and
infinitely attractive. You know that if an issue arises with
such a person it will be brought to the cross and the person
will conform to the cross. He will allow himself to be
crucified so that only the life of Christ will come through.
This, I say, is infinitely attractive and such people become
wonderfully attractive—not in themselves but through
Christ in them.

I started off by saying that you must make a clear
distinction. Christ knew us when He first came to us. He
knew us before He came. He knew us absolutely and He
distinguished between two states: He saw the people that
we were, and the people that we could be in Him, and
there is a tremendous difference between the two. He did
not love the sin. He did not love the fallen nature, but He
looked beyond the blemishes and the sin and saw essential
personality which was created to be filled with God. He
saw what we could be and I might almost say He loved us
into life. He re-created us in love.

I am going to give you a very simple illustration of this
principle from incidents which had a profound effect on
my life. I have given this often but I don't apologise for
doing so again. I came through two critical experiences in
my early days where love was concerned. I'm talking of
love in the 1 Corinthians 13 sense. I am not talking of
romantic love or anything of that kind. There was an
occasion when someone was very jealous of me and, I felt,
quite without justification. Jealousy, as you know, doesn't

always need justification. I was friendly with a second party and the person who was jealous coveted that friendship. I was not in competition but I ultimately became aware that the jealous person had spoken of me very disparagingly and unjustly to my friend. This person was a genuine friend and from him I discovered what was happening. As it happened I was in a position where, as the Americans might say, I could have fixed my enemy 'real good', and in these days it was a real pleasure to me to fix an enemy 'real good'. In fact I would have gone half across the world to get my own back on an enemy. I was born with a very keen sense of justice and I could take pleasure in revenge. That, of course, is not to my credit but I was born that way. I was a peaceful person but if you wanted to fight that was fine by me. I wouldn't start the fight but I would certainly try to end it. Anyway, here was the position and I had the cards, you might say, in my hand. But just at that time I was genuinely drawing near to God. I was really seeking Him deeply. I remember it as though it was yesterday. I was on the farm at home, carrying a couple of pails down to the piggery, and I was raging with anger at this man. The more I thought about the matter, the worse it got. I was like that: things started quietly but the more I thought about a grievance, the more anger rose up and up and up. And just in the very midst of this surging anger God spoke to me and said, 'Christ loves that man!' I didn't want to hear anything about that. But it was very strong as I proceeded on my way. I hadn't given in, but at least I was listening. I got maybe about twenty yards when He spoke again. 'Do you think you are better than Christ and have a right to hate that man whom He loves?' Now that stopped me in my tracks—that really shook me, and I gave in. God showed me, Christ showed me, that He loved that man in spite of the angering things He was doing to me. God loved him and God did not want me to be different from Christ and engage in a vendetta. I had to break.

God didn't tell me to love the sin in the man, to love the nastiness that I was being faced with, but He showed me a poor man. It was as though I saw a shrivelled creature, starved, almost invisible, but trying to come to life. There was something there that God loved, something there for which Christ had died. Christ loved that man. That poor sin-ridden, bound man—God loved him, Christ loved him and suddenly I saw it. Do you know, I began to love him too! Not what he was doing to me but the man himself, the man that Christ wanted. I saw the man he could become in Christ and it changed my whole attitude. I went and fed the pigs and forgot my anger.

The days passed, the months and the years passed and one day the same man came to my door. I was a teacher by that time and he had a son who was being treated very badly by a headmaster. The boy was a senior pupil and in those days you had to pass your subjects in not more than two sittings for University entrance. The headmaster was refusing to allow the boy to take his subjects in the necessary combination. The boy wanted to follow a particular profession and the father required advice. I dictated a letter and said, 'Put that in your own words and post it to the Director of Education and I think you'll find your boy will get the proper course.' He did just that and the boy was on the proper course within about forty-eight hours. I presume the headmaster would have a flea in his ear as well: he was really playing the fool. The man was absolutely delighted. He was thrilled. Was it a better thing that happened at the end than if I had taken cheap revenge in the earlier days? Anyway, all of the earlier business was wiped away and there was a lovely feeling left.

This story has just come up to date. A friend has told me this morning of a lady she met very recently who had been baptised in the Holy Spirit. Was she not a daughter of that same man, a sister of the lad whose course was corrected! How I do rejoice!

What did I learn? I learned to love, forgetting outward appearances, forgetting how people behaved and seeing through to that essential part of being that God wanted and that could be filled with God. An enemy could become a 'Christ person'. An enemy could be loved and that is what Christ did. He didn't just see what we were. He saw what we could be. There's a wonderful difference.

My second experience in this realm was much more severe and more painful. I had been baptised in the Spirit and my family (brothers and sisters) were terribly opposed to what had happened and to the line that I was teaching. Persecution rose and it was very, very painful, very grim. Those of you—and there are quite a number of you—who from time to time have deep family difficulty will understand. I am always sympathetic to those of you who have this kind of trial because I came through it very painfully indeed. One brother to whom I was close became particularly bitter. After I was baptised in the Spirit there came a terrible divide and real persecution. I am not going into the detail of all the things that happened but I know I suffered intensely. On one occasion when things had reached crisis point I went alone. I went on my knees and I knew I had to forgive. I knew I was not allowed to have a hard heart and harbour bitter feelings, but it seems that sometimes when God has got you to a particular place in His training He pushes you a bit further. To begin with He can be quite gentle but He wants His work completed and He made it very clear to me that He wasn't asking me merely to forgive my brother: He was asking me to love him. Now that seemed to me to be going a bit far in the circumstances. You know how you'll hear people say, 'Oh yes, I'll forgive, but I'll never forget.' You think, 'Well, forgiveness is a Christian duty. I'll do my best. I'll go on my knees and I'll say I have forgiven him.' God wasn't at all content with anything of that nature. He said, 'Love him,' and, oh, it was hard. The more I thought about it the harder it became (and I haven't got too sentimental a nature). You know how when somebody's annoying you—the more you think about it the worse it gets—and that's how things work in me naturally, until there comes an explosion point. Well, you can just imagine things beginning to boil in me. God said, 'Love him.' I was on my knees. I was alone and by God's grace I managed to do what I was told. Do you know that in the moment that love was born, that man totally lost all power to torment me, or to trouble me? I was totally free. I was living in another realm. He had no more power than a fly on the wall, and I suddenly realised something of the greatness of God and the power of love. I saw in the man a needy soul, prejudiced, hard, and I found that love was stronger than hatred.

Now this is the love of God. Get out of your head the notion that love is a matter of going to your brother and saying, 'Well, we'll shake hands, brother, and I'll give you an embrace and that's it.' It's far, far deeper than these external peripheral things. It's a deep down attitude. It is a quality that causes a person to be prepared to die for another, to give their whole life to a cause, to work to the end for others. Love is stronger than death.

We have a very foolish, fickle generation in many ways nowadays where this kind of thing is concerned. One of my daughters recently brought to my attention some of the late Professor Barclay's writings on the practice of 'greeting each other with a holy kiss.' He indicates that this was abandoned in the early Church for two reasons: first because of moral danger and second because of the criticism of unbelievers who suspected immorality. There are practices that can lower instinctive and natural barriers, and leave ways open for the flesh, but if you resist such practices you can sometimes be judged as aloof, cold and unloving. Now, mark, I am not suggesting for a moment that the embracing that goes on in Christian circles is immoral. I don't think that. I think a great deal of it hasn't got that overtone at all, but I do also think that for some people it can bring in that overtone. One has to be very careful in speaking about this. I am not saying that all of it is wrong but I am showing you that you can have a very deep flowing love that is not at all dependent on physical expression, and you can regard the physical expression as a sign of an overflowing love when it may be little more than mere custom. Try to distinguish. Try to look below the surface. The love of Christ can be very deeply experienced in a quite internal way. It may need no physical expression.

You will see that if Christ's love for us had depended on what we were or on how we behaved He would have forgotten us almost before He had begun to think about us. The love of Christ sees beyond what we are to what we may become. He sees beyond the human frailty to the Divine strength that may one day come flowing through us. He sees His own life and His own nature developing in us. His love for us carried Him right to the cross and for 'the joy that was set before Him He endured the cross, despising the shame, and sat down at the right hand of the Father'— a love that was unbreakable, a love that saw us not only as we were but as He wants us to be.

I remind you regularly that one of the main purposes of these teachings is to produce change. I can be a very down-to-earth person and I want to give you a direct challenge. If, as you go about your normal business, you suddenly discover that somebody has been talking about you behind your back, what is your reaction going to be? If someone plays you a dirty trick what is your reaction going to be? Is it going to be the Christ reaction of love taking no account of evil, or are you going to fight for your rights? Are you going to allow the deep change to take place in your nature whereby you become like Christ and allow none of these things to affect you or embitter you? Are you going to love? I have noticed that people who talk a lot about love and don't live it out are often very easily offended. Oh yes, you can tramp on their toes very easily. You can offend their pride very easily. You can wound their self-esteem when their conception of love is a carnal conception. When a soul is in deep love with God it is not trying just to win arguments or to win battles, it is out to win a war. Such a person takes an almost incredible amount of indignity against himself to win others for Christ. You are asked to be super-human. You are asked to enter the Divine, to share the Divine will and the Divine attitude. It is that love that took Christ to a cross. It is that love which wins the martyr's crown. It is that love which sustains the missionary through endless years of difficulty and trial. This is a love that is not born on earth: a love that is not earthy and that takes no account of evil, is not interested in self, self-aggrandisement, pride, position, but is totally self-effacing, totally giving—the love of Christ.

Are you prepared and willing to be changed? Be careful before you say that you don't need to be changed. What if someone sets a trap for you and tells you that a mutual friend has said a horrible thing about you: how will you react? Don't be too quick in claiming to be changed in the deeps. Don't be too quick to claim that you are dead to self. Dead bodies don't react at all, but I have observed that most Christian toes are very sensitive when stood upon. These matters are easily tested. It is only the saints, and they are real saints, who achieve the position of which I have spoken—and yet it is attainable by all of us.

Did you think from the title that you would have a pleasant study on the love of Christ? A discourse dripping with sentimentality on the love of Christ—concentrating on peripheral things regarding Christ? Go right to the heart of love. You will find it to be a wonderful but also an austere quality.

Compassion is its sister, so closely linked that it is difficult to deal with separately. Compassion to me is a wonderfully warm word. It has in it something of pity. It has in it a kindness, a consideration, a gentleness, an awareness of the needs and problems of others. It is a true sister of love.

We sometimes meet a situation where a person deserves a thorough dressing-down. He has asked for it very richly but as you look beyond him and see beneath the surface you have pity for him—there is compassion. First judgments should often be avoided or at least tempered. Sometimes you live to regret hasty actions that seem to be perfectly justified. Compassion pays, and often when firm action is required compassion is particularly necessary.

I remember the first boy I ever punished on becoming a headmaster. I look back on the incident with an element of amusement and an even stronger element of regret. Things were a bit slack when I took over the job. In fact, they were very slack. On this occasion a boy was brought to my door by a very angry teacher. My depute was in the office with me and they both came in. The boy had been filling his mouth with water and sloshing it all around him. You know what boys can be! It was a dirty boyish prank but he was refusing all punishment and he had a bad reputation. He was a big fellow with yellow hair hanging down to his shoulders, and he told me he wasn't taking punishment from me or from anybody else. My depute was being considerate of me since I was new to the job and he said, 'Mr .... (my predecessor) would read the code at this point.' I was of another mind and, having a poor opinion of the said code, replied, 'If you don't mind I'll read my own code this morning.' To the boy I said, 'Right, put your hands up!' (This was in the days of corporal punishment.) 'I'm no' taking it from you. I'm no' taking it from anybody!' he informed me. I then had to let him know that there was a difference between taking something and getting something and he was about to get something. My depute, maybe seeing a court case on the

horizon, slid out of the room leaving the teacher, myself
and junior (big junior!) alone. I'll draw a veil over the next
part of the proceedings. Suffice it to say that justice was
done and firm discipline administered. It was the beginning of the end of serious disobedience in the school. But
you know, I later discovered the home circumstances of
that boy and they really were fearful. He was living in a
hell on earth and somehow my enforcement of discipline
didn't seem quite so laudable as it had at first appeared. I
was sorry for that boy. I found I had compassion for him.
Now I don't mean that compassion should make you
foolishly soft, but it does cause you to be careful and to
take many things into account. I have never found that the
compassion of Christ makes for softness either. It makes
for a loving consideration and, if punishment is necessary,
then punishment is administered but it is administered in
love, never in bitterness. I wasn't administering it in bitterness—I never did that at any time—but I learned not
to forget compassion in pursuit of justice and discipline.

Have you ever noticed the iron in Christ, the firmness in
Christ? When I went into that school a prophetess had
quite a revelation—she told me things to come which were
in fact fulfilled and I was given a verse: 'I will make thy
forehead as adamant against their forehead.' Crime was
rife in the place and I felt that iron came into me as I
walked through the building. I felt as though a prowling,
evil beast was there. We met head on and incident after
incident took place until the opposition was totally broken, the insubordination, the indiscipline, the bullying,
the protection rackets, the crime. The iron of God came,
the iron of God. Love and iron go hand in hand. In our age
people think that love and softness go together, love and
slush. I tell you they don't. Love is strong, firm, powerful—a wonderful thing is love. There is no foolish softness
in it. There is no weakness in it. It is iron and it breaks the
bands of hell and sets the prisoners free.[1]

Well, would you like to have the love and the compassion of Christ and the iron firmness that drove men out of the temple and exposed the Pharisees as the hypocrites they were? He exposed them to the whole nation. His words of fire and power stung, and yet His was perfect love. A wonderful combination is seen in Christ, a combination very few people have ever understood. No stained-glass window, no milk and water picture of Christ, no weak effeminate face of Christ but iron character, love eternal. Strong enough to die for us. Or is my picture of Christ a different picture from yours?

Notes

[1] As a tailpiece to the school story you may be interested to know that in the six months prior to my taking up my appointment there had been eighty-three appearances of boys from the school in the local court. In the corresponding six months of the next year the number was down to sixteen and later it almost disappeared. The police noticed that the local incidence of crime was going against the national trend and on investigating discovered that this school's figures were the cause. The attention of psychologists was alerted and they wanted to know the reasons for the change. I lectured to a group of them but I am not at all sure that my method and their theories made good bed-fellows! I think they would like to have attributed success to an imaginative outdoor programme of activities which I had been running, while I emphasised that firm discipline at the centre was the real key.

I had discovered that amongst the boys it was the done thing to have a court appearance, and that a comparatively small core of real offenders exercised an undue influence on the potentially law-abiding section of the school. I set out to detach one group from the other. This was fairly easily done. To have a court offence or seriously break school rules earned detention and so 'The Four O'Clock Club' was formed. Each evening as school was dismissed the bulk of the pupils saw their erstwhile heroes at their desks in the detention room and somehow they did not seem so great.

Most parents were pleased, but there could be an occasional query. They found it difficult, however, to argue against the reasonableness of the sentence passed on their offending offspring—namely: 'In order to enable you to fit into your social context, you are being given an hour's extra tuition each evening quite free of charge in this instance.'

Who could resist a good bargain like that? There was no talk of punishment, simply enrichment. Junior understood, however. Junior understood perfectly. Law and order were restored.

Perhaps I could give one illustration. One lad had been guilty of vandalising eleven car aerials prior to coming into our school. He was on the roll, however, before his case came before the Children's Panel. As soon as I heard about the matter I put him on detention on the ground that he was bringing disgrace to the school although he had not been a pupil when the offences occurred. His father, who was a very reasonable man, came to see me and thought my action was a bit extreme. I pointed out to him that in the normal course of things his boy would appear before the Children's Panel and nothing significant would happen to him there. He would come away with the feeling that he could get away with breaking the law. By being too lightly punished boys often became hardened in crime and when serious offences took place it was often difficult to change the pattern. I said, 'We would be wise to be very firm with this boy right at the beginning of his wrongdoing. The traumatic shock of firm handling will very possibly prevent him going any further on the wrong road.' I put it in strong terms and asked the father to support me in the action and be equally firm at home. The father listened carefully and concurred. That boy never crossed my path again for any offence great or small. The psychologists may not fully agree with the methods but actually they work!

5

Self-effacement and God-centredness

Self-effacement and God-centredness are the next areas for our consideration. You will remember that I have taken the qualities of peace and tranquillity, purity and serenity, strength and courage, love and compassion. We are now approaching the end of the series and the selection of these two qualities may surprise you. As you know I did not feel I chose the qualities or the order in which they have come. Both the subjects and their order seemed to present themselves in a moment of time. I jotted them down, noting that they tended to be in pairs. The last two, you may feel, are an unusual choice—*self-effacement and God-centredness*. You will notice that they also are a natural pair and I can hardly speak of one without involving the other. I will start with self-effacement.

This presents us with difficulty—not difficulty in understanding the qualities but rather difficulty in attaining them. Christ had no problems with self-effacement or God-centredness, but we do. We see these qualities in Christ and realise that God wants us to be like Him and have the qualities which are revealed in Him, to change us from what we are to what we ought to be, to have Christ live out His life in power within us.

It is not enough for us to say, 'I like that, it appeals to me, I understand that.' We come to the point where the qualities we admire in Him must become ours. We must change from 'glory to glory as we behold His face'. First we change from what we are to what we can be in Him. His life enters into us and radiates and emanates from us. We must change. If we cannot change, why preach? If I do not believe that this change can take place, why speak about it? What is the point? What is the point of being admirers of the life of God and the beauties of Christ for ever from afar? 'Oh, isn't it wonderful! Wasn't it a wonderful sermon? Wasn't it this and wasn't it that?' But is it in you? Is it in me? Is it affecting us now? Is it changing us? Is it producing the life of Christ in us?

Speaking reverently, I suggest that God may not be nearly so interested in what we think as in what we are and what we do. Oh, we are wonderfully educated in this and that—so what? What *are* we? Not just what are our ideas, but what are we who have the ideas? He wants to change us—to *change* us.

Self-effacement . . . . Immediately we go tumbling into the pit when we begin to think of self-effacement. A lot of folks think that self-effacement is a kind of mock humility—a Uriah Heep-ness.

It reminds me of a Highland lady who came home from Church. They had a new minister and 'Oh, he was wonderful! It was wonderful! A wonderful sermon!' Somebody said, 'What was he preaching about? What did he say?' She gave the questioner a withering look, 'And how would you be expecting a poor ignorant woman like me to be able to understand the likes of a great man like that?' A typical Highland response!

Actually you get a good deal of hypocrisy in some Christian circles. 'You will remember to pray for me. I am a poor, poor soul. I am so humble. I can hardly stand on my own two feet.' And they are not one little bit humble. You can get a mock humility that is for ever indulging in self-denigration while concealing rampant pride. Basically the person is thinking, 'I am really wonderful but it is the done thing to pretend not to be at all wonderful. I must appear to be humble.' So a great big cloak of humility is put on but unfortunately it bulges all over and discerning people see the true character which it is supposed to hide. Now God has no time at all for the wearing of this grotesque cloak of self-denigration, this false refusing of a man to take account of himself as he ought. There is no place in the Kingdom for people who are playing this kind of game, and oddly enough mock humility shows and shows very clearly. It is so different from real humility. Mock humility has nothing to do with self-effacement.

And then of course at the other end of the scale there are people who are unashamedly proud. They may even be proud of being proud and don't care who knows it. They vaunt themselves. They may have all three aspects of pride of which I often speak: pride of face, pride of place, and pride of grace. The pride of face is so obviously foolish for in time it comes to a sad end. To cover the deficiencies the ladies may resort to paint and powder when they are past the first fair flush of youth, so you will realise we may assume the latter if we see the former! Seriously, as old age comes on the pride of face becomes particularly inappropriate. The pride of place is perhaps even worse. There is a more spiritual side to that. You can sense the attitude. A man gets a new job. It affects the way he walks. He struts around. It can be very funny! I won't go into the detail of it. Possibly the pride of grace is the worst of all. This is a serious and a dangerous pride. Was it not because of such pride that Satan fell? A horrible pride!

Consider Christ. You see in Him perfection. He knew exactly Who He was. He knew Whom He represented. He never played Himself down. Nothing false was ever found in Christ (I hate even to use the word 'false' in speaking

His name)—there was no shadow of falsity in Him either in His estimate of Himself or of other people. You never sense in Him the slightest touch of pride, the slightest touch of a human kind of ambition—rather a perfection of self-effacement. This is very difficult to define, to analyse. It is very difficult to convey the flavour of this quality and I recommend you to re-read the Gospels. Come close to the Christ in action. You then feel and sense the quality rather than have a mere intellectual understanding of it. It is a 'felt' thing. You become God-conscious as you meet Christ. You become conscious of the Divine. You become conscious of perfection and you are able to pick up from some of the things He did and refrained from doing, something of the innerness of the quality. For example, you find that at the end of a particularly wonderful day of ministry, with the sick healed, perchance the dead raised, the storm stilled, the loaves multiplied, you never get a breath of a thought that Christ sits down and calls the twelve and says, 'Now, didn't I do that wonderfully well?' The very thought is anathema. What do you find? You don't find Him waiting in the wings to hear a complimentary comment. You picture Him rather withdrawing from the crowd, going alone into a desert place, going up the mountain alone with God, totally unmoved by the praise of men, or by the blame of men—not looking for the compliments of men. What about us? When it comes down to bedrock, so many of us love compliments. We love the plaudits of men, we love to be well thought of, and you'll find that preachers are not exempt. May I speak to you as an older leader? I will tell you some of the pitfalls that lie along this road.

If you are moving under the power of God there are certain things you may notice. You will notice that when His power is on you there comes an amazing clarity. It can be in personal counselling for salvation. It can be in preaching. It can be in any of the ministries. There just comes a tremendous grip, a control, a sense of God. God grips and you find that words become like arrows and they find their mark. You say the right thing to the right person at the right time. You are explaining the gospel and it's so wonderfully simple that you feel you never noticed before the clarity or the directness yourself. Before you are properly off the platform there may come a voice in your ear, 'You know, you did that very well tonight!' Watch that voice. The voice of Satan comes very insidiously. You know you might say, 'Well, I did do very well tonight.' *You* didn't do very well at all. The Holy Spirit had control of you for a little time and He did wonderfully well. *You* didn't, you know! You were dependent on Him and in so far as *He* did it, it was perfect. None of the praise belongs to you. None of the credit is yours at all. You happened to be the vessel that He picked up to use, but Satan would intervene and say, 'You really are quite a fellow. You know you are really very useful. You are doing these things very well. You are coming along famously.' You think, 'Well, maybe, maybe . . .' and that is just about the end.

I don't understand this exactly, but there are certain red lights that you find in life. I found one in this area many years ago, and this has never changed. I don't know why it is so important but it is extremely so. You must never put out your hand to touch the glory of God. You must never take to yourself that which belongs to Him. It is an extreme sin. It's not a small sin. It's not a peripheral matter. It is a sin of the spirit that can wound you and I think affect you profoundly. Never touch the glory of God. You have been pleased with your preaching. I tell you, if *He* did it, *He* did it: if *He* didn't do it, be ashamed of yourself. One thing is sure, if it was under His power *you* didn't do it, and to take the credit is to try to steal that which is His. Satan will say *you* did it. You are a fine fellow. To accept this is serious sin. Never be caught on this particular hook. (On that point, as I said, I saw a red light from days almost beyond my memory.) Don't even consider Satan's suggestion. Don't agree with it and then repent of it. From the very moment the first of these words are being addressed to your spirit throw them out. Throw them out totally! Don't think about them. Don't consider them. Never see yourself as important, as having done well, as having become a great person. Forget it completely.*

You may listen to me, but human nature is very slow to learn this. It touches a deep level, a hidden level; and people can blind themselves to it. In the deeps of your spirit you can sin and say, 'In spite of what he says, I *am* special. I have got something unique and I am particular. In spite of what he says I *am* a cut above other people.' Nobody with natural eyes sees into the depth of the heart. Those with spiritual eyes can see all right and pride is normally extremely obvious. There must be truth in the inner parts. There must be true humility.

Humility shouldn't really be so very difficult. All you need is a dash of honesty. Those of you who are leaders and preachers will know, and perhaps none better, how you would like to stand on a platform without the anointing, without the Presence of God. You only need to recollect an instance in which that may have happened to know just what an abject specimen you really are. Left to yourself you would bore yourself, never mind the congregation. There's no future in it at all and if you are honest you realise that if you are successful, God is successful, not you. Left to yourself you are nothing, a nobody. So all you need is just a little bit of honesty to realise that you have nothing to boast of, nothing at all.

---

* I like article 57 of the Benedictine rule which directed that if a monk became proud of his work he had to give it up.

Oh, this way doesn't suit the flesh, does it? This teaching never lets you get up at all—never lets you become important. Dear, dear, a terrible way is this, the way of God! Me never to be anything? No, not ever anything at all—not ever: never. I'm not even allowed to think, 'Oh well, I'll get expanding when I get to Heaven. I'll be important then!' You'll not, you know.

It's good to come to terms with this conception right at the very beginning. It's not a temporary crucifixion which God is putting you through. It is for ever—the old fallen part never to live again! The old, proud, ambitious, self-seeking part never to revive again! Never at all, never at any time or place. It is a total death and the flesh hates it. It hates it intensely. It wants to achieve something sometime. Well, it isn't to get anything for itself ever—save death. Of course this isn't really death. It is life, but we'll not go into that in depth now. Suffice for the moment to say that our true selves transformed in Christ live forever. In that sense there is no death. Darkness is swallowed up in light, sin in righteousness and defeat in victory.

So in considering self-effacement I came to the point of giving a little advice about certain danger areas, about the voice that can sound, 'You did that quite well.' This is to be rejected and resisted from the beginning. I now find that the two subjects self-effacement and God-centredness run almost inextricably into each other. In successful ministry you are dependent on the action of God and you forget all about self-effacement or self-advertisement, or self in any sense of the word, and the source of life is God. You actually forget about yourself. You neither push yourself, nor exalt yourself, nor denigrate yourself. You just treat yourself as though you weren't there, as though there was no self. That is how to deal with self. You neither try to talk it down nor talk it up—you just ignore it, just live as though there was no self. As you go into situations, emanate God. As people meet you when you are selflessly living in God they too may find God. They are not conscious of you. They don't go away from a service thinking, 'That was a great preacher.' They go away thinking, 'God is great. God is wonderful. The things that God does are wonderful,' and they remember, 'Yes, there was a mouthpiece but I wasn't particularly interested in the mouthpiece. I was interested in what was coming through that mouth. I was interested in the emanation of Christ. I felt the life of Christ there.' The true man of God doesn't draw people to himself. He draws people to God. He leaves them with a consciousness of God.

In Christian work there are many difficulties that can rise. In early stages people do need help, and like a child leaning on a human parent so a spiritual child very properly draws life from spiritual channels and he associates blessing with these channels. That is very understandable. It is allowed; it is right; but there comes a subtle point where you have to be very, very careful. The child must be weaned. Now the unscrupulous leader draws people to himself. He encourages the development of a wrong relationship. He encourages others to go on depending on him for spiritual life. Never do that. Never draw people to yourself. Hold people for God until the point comes where they can draw directly from God Himself. Do not allow them to become dependent on you in a wrong way, and when they develop their own relationship with God their relationship with you will actually deepen but it will not be a wrongly dependent relationship. Avoid for ever the personality cult. Do not encourage people to lean on *people*. Quickly get them to a place of leaning on God alone. Build your relationships in Christ and not directly one with another. Guard the relationships God gives you with each other. Neither add to them nor take from them. Accept them. That way you will find that your relationships can be perfect.

God-centredness. Think of Christ. From the very beginning He was about His Father's business. From the very beginning He was speaking of God. In His earthly ministry He was revealing God. He was showing the innerness of Divine truth—the innerness—not just the periphery of the law; the innerness of the marriage relationship and what it had originally been. He was forever taking people through to God. As you read of Christ you quickly realise that His own life was immersed in God. He could say, 'I do nothing of myself, but whatsoever I see the Father do, that do I.' Totally God-dependent, totally God-centred.

There is a truth which I often emphasise when preaching on the Baptism in the Spirit. I find that many people are largely self-dependent. They don't really want to be fully and completely controlled by God. For me it was a remarkable day when I first realised that we never read that Christ performed a miracle on the ground of His deity, although one tends to think in these terms. I discovered that the Bible teaches that His miracles were performed by the power of the Holy Spirit. I realised that upon that Holy One at Jordan the Holy Spirit came down and He was dependent on the Holy Spirit. Now if He, the perfect, the holy and the pure was God-dependent, how can you or I ever hope to work the works of God in our own strength? How can we possibly even imagine it? Do you know the road that opened to Him opens to us—a total dependency on the Spirit of God, literally? If we can find it, we'll share His life. We will be God-centred.

Many people come to me not just at Conference and Camp time but in the course of normal church life (if there is such a thing as normal church life). Many come in deep need, some in desperate need. There is nobody more aware than I am that I can't meet your need at all—whether for salvation, Baptism in the Spirit, exorcism, healing or anything else, and yet you come and you are met in so many cases. What happens? What happens?

Perhaps I could illustrate it from the first case of the Baptism in the Spirit in which I was ever used. I had many false starts in earlier days because it was the 'done thing' for everybody to lay on hands and sometimes with unhappy consequences. I had never so far as I know really been used in anybody's Baptism prior to this occasion, but God revealed to me that day an inner secret as I laid on hands. I was myself lost in God. The Holy Spirit was poured out and the man on whom my hands rested began to be baptised. I saw what was happening and began to concentrate on the man. As I did so power tended to depart. Then I remembered it was as I was lost in God that the power had flowed. So I got lost in God again and the power returned. The man was wonderfully baptised in the Holy Spirit that night. Man can do nothing in this realm. The power forever comes from God.

You lay hands on people and they begin to speak in tongues. Oh, glory be to God! Praise the Lord! . . . And you become interested in what they are doing and it suddenly stops. Continue to be interested in Him and what He is doing and it goes on and on. Immerse yourself in God, not in the surface of things that are visible to the human eye and audible to the human ear. You are to be God-centred, lost in God and not taken up with the externals of life.

Some of you will find the next part difficult, to begin with. If I am involved in exorcism and a body is thrashing around on the floor like a writhing snake you may say, 'But you are bound to be interested and how can you help being involved?' Not really. It doesn't matter how many snakes there are in the world and how much they are writhing. It is of no significance whatever from one point of view. Forget all about the snake. That has nothing to do with you. What has to do with you is the living God. You concentrate on the living God and He deals with the snakes and before you know where you are it is all over. They are gone, finished. If you get personally involved with the operation you may be there all day and be in a bad state at the end of it. But if you are involved with Him it's wonderful.

You have to watch carefully in the realm of exorcism. Quite often the demons speak, you see, and would cause you to be taken up with what they've got to say. Well, the opinions of demons should not be regarded. They are often steeped in lies. I can, for instance, be right in the midst of an exorcism when the demons shout at me (and I often shout back) but I don't become unduly concerned or taken up with what they've got to say. I have known them scream at me as they go out that they'll be back and sure enough if the person is not careful and returns to the sin that caused the entrance, they may very well be back.

There was one case that shook me—the one to which I referred in another context where the person informed me right in the midst of exorcism of a rising desire to plunge back into the sin which had caused the condition. I didn't know what to do until Christ came in a particular way and dealt gloriously with the situation. My attention, I suppose, may have come off Him and on to the problem. Basically we have one thing in life to do and that is to obey God and to allow Him to be in control. It is not what *we* do but what *He* does that is important.

In a recent meeting a theme very close to my heart was touched on. People think that they have a right to argue things out. People think they have a right to think. Someone recently wrote many thousands of words to me and I have just learned that he has sent me another letter and will be looking for endless answers. He expects to get solutions through talking, explaining, understanding. Now there is a realm in which it is proper to talk and explain and understand but there is also a time not to talk and if the Spirit signals, 'Say nothing,' that is the course to follow. Sometimes God just says bluntly, 'I am not going to tell you.' 'But . . . but . . . but . . . but . . . .' No 'buts' about it. God will often say that to you in life. 'But I would like to know!' You are not necessarily entitled to know. It's not always His will to tell you things. He sometimes reveals them later, sometimes He does not.

In the innerness of spiritual life you walk with God and you speak or refrain from speaking as the Spirit indicates. You say, 'That's too hard a way for me.' It isn't really, you know. Sometimes God says, 'No more on that point.' If so, end it there. You may feed an obsession. You may cause a condition in another person to worsen by endless talking. You need to be sensitive to that Voice. A person may say, 'But I can't take this teaching.' 'Well,' you reply, 'I cannot go beyond the command of God and you may have to learn to take it, to learn to deny your obsession, to learn to hear the voice of the Spirit and to obey Him only.' It's difficult to get people out of the flesh and into the Spirit. It has been said it was easier to get Israel out of Egypt than it was to get Egypt out of Israel. I sometimes think it is easier to get people out of positively anti-Pentecostal churches than it is to get mistaken traditions and prejudices out of these same people when they come out. It is difficult to be fully and continuously God-controlled.

You can fill in the other stretches for yourself. God-centredness in everything that comes in life. Think of Christ in this particular way—through Gethsemane, the trial scenes and the cross. He endured as seeing Him Who is invisible—centred on God. 'Thou wilt keep him in perfect peace whose mind is stayed on Thee.' 'Come up higher.'

I do trust that the qualities of Christ have been attractive to you. Oh to be like Him: to have His peace, tranquillity, purity, serenity, strength, courage, love, compassion, self-effacement, God-centredness. To be like Jesus!

6

The Power and the Glory

This chapter has been added with a view to publication of
the whole. It did not form part of the initial series of
addresses but as I prepared these for printing I felt that
there was something incomplete. While power had been
mentioned in an earlier chapter it had not been included as
one of the ten qualities principally highlighted. A consideration of *power and glory* seems a fitting way in which to
conclude the series.

Because of Christ's humility and self-effacement,
undiscerning people do not always immediately sense His
power. He moved quietly amongst men. There was no
bombast with Him, no boastfulness—no attempt to
impress or dominate in human ways. He was 'meek and
lowly of heart', a gentle person.

Foolish men often associate power with outward show
and display—with noise and bombast. Natural power is
often coupled with self-assertiveness. In the spiritual
realm things are so very different. Spiritual things are
spiritually judged and the power of Christ was an intensely
spiritual thing. I am reminded of Hudson Taylor, the
founder of the China Inland Mission. One lady had long

desired to meet him and at long last he was to be her guest for a few days. He arrived and she was greatly disappointed. He was so quiet and unassuming. There was no suggestion about him that 'God's man for the hour' had arrived. There was no attempt to dominate or impress. He was so natural, but also kind and considerate. Gradually she became aware of his true quality. In a comparatively short time she almost wondered if it was an angel from Heaven who had come to her home. His Christlikeness shone so brightly.

Because of His deep inner quietness, power may not have been the first quality of which men became aware when meeting Christ, but it is very obvious from the gospel records that His power soon affected them profoundly.

It is sometimes good to stand back from a situation with which we are familiar and try to view it objectively. In considering the life of Christ we can have an overall impression—but when we turn the searchlight on to the individual qualities, things assumed, but not always closely observed, begin to emerge. When we focus our attention on power in isolation the revelation can be startling. He walked as a man amongst men, in meekness and humility but—

He taught with power and authority and not as the scribes and Pharisees. He revealed inner truth and His teaching profoundly affected men in His own day and through all succeeding ages.

He deferred to no man. He followed His own path, turning neither to left nor right through fear of man or for praise or blame. His courage was absolute.

He defended the weak and needy and unhesitatingly denounced hypocritical religious leaders who made their burdens heavy. With a seven-fold woe he publicly branded the scribes and Pharisees at the risk of His life.

He healed all manner of sicknesses and diseases: the lame walked; the deaf heard; the blind saw; the crippled were made whole; the insane were restored to their right minds. He did this in various ways by a word, by a touch, by being touched, by exercising His own faith, by calling forth the faith of others.

He cast out demons.

He raised the dead.

He demonstrated His power over nature, multiplying food miraculously and turning water into wine. He stilled the storm at a word. Immediately at His command the winds obeyed. He walked on water.

It is little wonder that His disciples could exclaim, 'Behold, what manner of man is this?' They had witnessed His miracles in many spheres, but seemingly the fact that the winds and waves obeyed His voice was too much for them. They were astounded and so they might well be! And so may we!

We tend to become familiar with at least some of the effects of Christ's work and it is good to stand back from the canvas and view the scene afresh. Others have gloriously indicated how profound His effect has been on history. He has divided time itself into B.C. and A.D. He was born in an obscure corner of a subjugated land, followed by a small uneducated group of disciples who deserted Him in death, crucified as a felon by the Roman authority. He wrote no book, founded no college, and yet His influence has been greater far than that of any other. As one has said, 'All the armies that ever marched, all the navies that ever sailed, have not influenced the lives of men as much as that one solitary life.' No poet, writer, politician, statesman, general or monarch has ever been His equal. Well might Napoleon conclude in exile on St. Helena, as he viewed the ruins of his own life, that whereas he had founded his empire on military might, Christ had founded His on love. Napoleon had reached his throne over the broken bodies of men; Christ had given His own body to be broken. Napoleon had spilled seas of blood to gain his empire; Christ had shed His own blood to found His. Pondering the past, well might the great general exclaim, 'Today there is not a sword in Europe that would be unsheathed for me, yet millions would gladly die for Him. Can this indeed be the Christ?' Indeed yes! Who else? Who else?

As we view His life we become increasingly aware of His power. It astonished His followers. It confounded His enemies who could not deny the miraculous, but some of whom attributed the power to the devil, thereby receiving Christ's fearful warning about unpardonable sin. No man could deny the power of Chirst, but what is perhaps more remarkable is the effect which His very presence had on demons. When ordinary people moved amongst the demon-possessed the latter were unaffected. Religious leaders, scholars, scribes, Pharisees, Sadducees might all pass by with no effect, but when He came—that one so quiet and kindly, so gentle and so compassionate—these evil entities cried out in terror. 'We know Thee who Thou art, Thou Holy One of God. Art Thou come to torment us before our time?' This was remarkable and we should deeply ponder its implications. In the spiritual world the force of Christ was phenomenal. He radiated power. Foolish men might but dimly perceive it, but demon entities recognised it and feared exceedingly. They knew the reality of it. Does this not have a humbling effect on us? As we move amongst men, do the demons fear and cry out, or do they remain where they are in peace and continue to torment their victims? 'Let the oppressed go free!' is still the command of Christ, and the responsibility is ours.

I have always found it wonderful and somewhat startling that without outward demonstration Christ should have had such an effect on demons—even without His speaking one word. What caused them such profound disturbance? He was so gentle. I believe His presence spelled hell to them. I have often thought that there is a sense in which hell is the other side of Heaven. For an unclean soul to draw near to Heaven is very hell. For unclean spirits to find themselves near Christ brought intolerable pain. It was not simply that they recognised Him and were reminded of their ultimate destiny. It was rather that they felt the very fire of hell in the presence of His holiness. Would to God that we had more holy men today so to disturb the kingdom of darkness and 'bind the strong man.'

Now it is one thing to recognise and glory in the power of Christ but surely there is a further stage. Surely His power has further relevance for us. Can we share that power? May we too know its wonderful operation? Let us go directly to Scripture—to His own words. On resurrection ground He declared, 'All authority (power: AV) hath been given unto me in heaven and on earth. Go ye therefore and make disciples of all the nations, baptizing them into the name of the Father and of the Son and of the Holy Ghost . . .' (Mt 28:18–19) and again, 'But ye shall receive power when the Holy Ghost is come upon you; and ye shall be my witnesses both in Jerusalem, and in all Judaea and Samaria, and unto the uttermost part of the earth' (Acts 1:8). It is His will that we should receive His power. Indeed He forbade the early disciples to leave Jerusalem until they had received it, which, in fact, they did on the day of Pentecost.

We now come to a point of great importance in our study of power in relation to the life of Christ—a point which many fail to notice and to which I have referred earlier. In my own case I had been keenly aware of Christ's power, had myself been baptised in the Holy Spirit and had sought to serve God, but had failed to see the significance of the relationship between the Lord Jesus Christ and the Holy Spirit. There come times in life when truth dawns on the soul and it is like a sunburst. Things are never the same again. A new dawn has arisen. A profound truth has been revealed. Like many more I had gone through life thinking of Christ as not only the Son of God, but as God the Son. Subconsciously, I suppose, I considered that He performed His miracles on the ground of His deity. He was different from us. He was Divine.

Suddenly I saw that He moved and ministered by the power of the Spirit. He could say, 'I do nothing of Myself, but whatsoever I see the Father do, that do I.' I was profoundly affected by these considerations, and let me emphasise again: If He, the Holy One of God, should be so dependent on the Holy Spirit, what folly would it be for me to hope to work the works of God in my own strength. Nor would it be in order for me to try to work with God or try to wield the power of God. The conception is quite different. It is the glory of *being moved by* the power of God—of that power being in action through human channels. This is the power that changes the world. This is the power that Christ wants to let loose amongst men. He rejoiced in His going back to the Glory since the Comforter, the Holy Spirit, would then come and be with His followers for ever.

He said, 'Greater works than these shall ye do.' In the days of His flesh, the Holy Spirit worked through Him mightily—through one body, two hands, two feet, one head, one tongue, one heart. The day was to come when that same Holy Spirit would move through myriad hands, myriad feet, myriad tongues, myriad hearts—through the Church, the Body of Christ.

I am aware that in my preaching and writing I return again and again to the theme of death to self and total dependency on the Holy Spirit. The position exemplified in the life of Christ seems to me to be of such fundamental importance and yet seems seldom to be noticed. In my view, most people never enter into the inner secret of the position and are forever the poorer as a result. Those who do find the door are phenomenally used of God.

As we ponder the power of Christ our attention becomes focused on the Holy Spirit. Can I emphasise sufficiently our need to be possessed by Him, and I mean 'possessed'. At conversion we are born of Him. He then 'abides' with us. 'But,' said Christ to His disciples, 'He shall be in you.' It was not enough to have Him abiding with them. He was to be in them. Nor should we view this in a vague general way. He is to be in us as a possessing power. Yes, 'possessing'—fully 'possessing'. Few seriously consider this, far less experience it. Many are baptised in the Spirit with signs following—but few live constantly under the power and leave themselves continually open for complete possession. This is a glorious way—a glorious possibility. The few who find the way are wonderfully and miraculously used of God. For a man to be really possessed by demon power is a fearful thing—but do not let the fear which rises from this prevent you opening yourself without reservation to full possession by Holy power. It is your destiny in the will of God. It may be that God anticipated this very fear in the hearts of men and made provision for us. Christ said: 'Ask, and it shall be given you; seek, and ye shall find; knock, and it shall be opened unto you: for every one that asketh receiveth; and he that seeketh findeth; and to him that knocketh it shall be opened. Or what man is there of you, who, if his son shall ask him for a loaf, will give him a stone; or if he shall ask for a fish, will give him a serpent? If ye then, being evil, know how to give good gifts unto your children, how much more shall your Father which is in heaven give good things to them that ask him?'

God, in Christ, became man and God moved through that man to bring a world back to Himself. God was the author and finisher of the work of redemption. God is ultimately all in all. Away then with any and all works of the flesh. God does not need our help. Let human endeavour cease. Let us assume our rightful place—as recipients of Divine life and power—that He may work His works through us. It is all so simple yet so profound. For me the dawning of this truth has had life-changing significance. There comes a conscious reliance on the Holy Spirit and ministry is profoundly affected.* Duncan Campbell of Lewis revival fame used to say, 'In revival men become God-conscious.' As revival draws near some of us are becoming increasingly God-conscious. Man and man's works are forgotten. God begins to fill the horizon. This will be increasingly so as we move into the last great days before Christ's coming again. The consciousness of God is coming into the atmosphere. It is His presence that will change and transform the lives of men as the last great revival comes in like a flood.

Power and authority. Often the words are used interchangeably, but there can be a shade of difference in meaning. Not only did Christ have the power of God flowing through Him but He had authority from God to do His works. In a similar way we do not go out by our own choice to work for God. We receive a commission from Him. We go out at His command. We receive our authority to operate from Himself. In human affairs an official may take certain actions and be required to furnish proof of his authority for so doing. This may be confirmed in a document which can be produced. The right is vested in the issuing authority. In our case the authority is God Himself. He commissions us in the sphere in which He wishes us to operate. Christ could say, 'All authority (a particular meaning of power) is mine—go ye therefore into all the world and preach the gospel.' He authorised the mission of His disciples and He also gave power over

---

* This subject is further discussed in *Reflections on the Gifts of the Spirit* with reference to the ministries of Kathryn Kuhlman and David Wilkerson.

all the power of the enemy. He does precisely the same with us in our day.

Glory. Who shall define or describe the glory of Christ? John could say, 'And we beheld his glory, glory as of the only begotten of the Father, full of grace and truth.' We read about being changed from glory unto glory as we behold His face. But what is His glory? It is the shining forth of His essential being—an emanation of unsullied purity and light—an attribute of deity. 'Father,' He could pray, 'glorify Thou Me with the glory I had with Thee before the world was,' and again, 'that they may behold My glory, which Thou hast given Me.' The very word glory takes us heavenward. It carries a flavour, an aura, almost a sensation as of something felt and yet remaining beyond our powers of comprehension or description. 'Now we see in a glass darkly.' There on the mount of transfiguration when 'His garments became glistering, exceeding white; so as no fuller on earth can whiten them' surely there was a shining of His glory—though no doubt dimmed, else the disciples would not have lived. Even the reflection of the glory of God from the face of Moses in an earlier day had to be veiled, so intense was its shining. In the intense glory of Divine majesty no man could survive. Of God we read, 'He is light,' and He dwells 'in light unapproachable; whom no man hath seen nor can see.' From the book of Hebrews we learn that Christ is 'the effulgence (or outshining) of His glory, and the very image of His substance' and in Him dwells 'all the fulness of the Godhead bodily.' The glory of Christ is the glory of God.

In the garden of Gethsemane, as we have seen, there was an outflashing of His glory. 'Whom seek ye?' he said to the soldiers who came to arrest Him. On his reply they fell back as dead men. But He veiled His glory and His power, and for our sakes allowed Himself to be taken. We often refer to the glory of the resurrection—but what of His ascension glory? Perhaps it is best described by John in the

Book of Revelation. John was a prisoner on the Isle of Patmos and found himself in the Spirit on the Lord's day. Suddenly he heard a voice and saw the Lord. The vision of that glory was too much for him. In the years of Christ's earthly ministry John had been very close to Him and loved Him dearly. Indeed there had been a special bond between them. John refers to himself as the disciple whom Jesus loved. It was John who leaned back on His breast at the last supper. There is no leaning now. Christ is in ascension glory and although His face shines as 'the sun shineth in his strength' the glory is still veiled. John falls at His feet as one dead. Oh the glory of Christ! Truly, we will not appear in that Presence lightly, familiarly, casually; but with tremendous awe. The glory of Christ. And yet I feel visual terms do not fully describe that glory. It is a quality. It almost has substance. It is an atmosphere, a tingling joy of victory, an overcoming, a well-being, a delirious happiness of spirit. It is glory – just glory!

Ours it is to share. We are His bride, His beloved. His glory is ours. Shall we enter in?

In my view there is, in the immediate Presence of God, such a weight of glory and intensity of power that no mortal could come anywhere near and live unless there was a veiling. In the Holy of Holies the cherubim and seraphim had to cover their faces, and the tabernacle was but a shadow of things in the heavenlies. If the Presence of God was so intense on earth, what must it be like in the heavenlies on which the earthly tabernacle was patterned? When Solomon's temple was dedicated the glory that came down was so great that the priests could not minister. Christ passed through the heavens into Heaven itself and sat down on the right hand of the Majesty on high, and dying Stephen saw him there, his own face shining as the face of an angel. Oh yes, there is glory on ahead! There is glory here and now. He who finds Christ finds glory, and he who enters deeply into His life enters deeply into His glory. It is there for us now and it is His will that we enter in.

Surely, as we view not only the power and the glory but the other qualities of Christ considered earlier, we needs must fall down and worship Him, declaring in the words of another, 'He is the altogether lovely one, the chiefest among ten thousand'; or perchance if we are given a deeper entrance to that Holy Presence we will, like John of old, fall in silence at His feet 'as one dead'.

7

But How Can I Be Like Him?

It has been suggested that I should add a further chapter to this book to round things off and give instruction on the subject of change. I feel there is wisdom in this and have complied. I have emphasised and re-emphasised in these chapters that the fundamental purpose of the teaching is not merely to give intellectual enlightenment but to produce change in the hearts and lives of the followers of Christ. But someone will ask, 'How can I change?' It is a very down to earth, practical question and it must be answered at that level. Preaching and teaching often leave people bemused and unable to apply principles to daily life simply because they don't know how to do it.

Now in secular matters great care is taken to bring theory into the realm of practice as, for example, in the world of commerce. There are theories of production and distribution and the people concerned in the various areas are given very clear and practical instruction in the ways in which they are to fulfil their roles. Little is left to chance— money is involved and money is regarded as important. But in the affairs of God we are often much more vague and general and we do not always take care to ensure that people actually know how to put theory into practice. Frequently in meetings I conclude the preaching part by saying, 'You have heard the theory. Let us now proceed to the practice.' I may have been speaking about salvation or Baptism in the Spirit or exorcism. I then expect the unsaved to be saved, the unbaptised believers to be filled with the Spirit, the demon-possessed to be set free. In God's view, I believe, successful action is generally the goal of preaching. Preaching is not an end in itself.

So how do people change? Let me first say that one of the distinctive features of Christianity is that it changes people. The doctrine assumes that men need to be changed and that they can be changed. It does not grant salvation on the ground of mere head knowledge of doctrine. It demands a change and produces a change. Now this is remarkable, for normally the lines of character form in very early life and seldom really change much. People's habits change, their views change, but they themselves seldom radically alter. Surly dispositions remain: cheerful temperaments continue. Changes are infrequent. But then comes Christ and He offers to change people or rather He demands that people change. In some cases from being self-centred, selfish, sinful, disobedient to God and His laws, they become God-centred, caring for others, holy, obedient. From being down-trodden, despondent, depressed, despairing, suicidal, they become overcomers, cheerful, happy, hopeful and full of life. They change. Now this is really quite wonderful. Not only does He make the beggar a priest and a king—he makes him a different person inside. Other religions don't do this. It is a marked feature of Christianity:

> From glory to glory You're changing me,
>   Changing me—You're transforming me;
> From glory to glory You're changing me,
>   How wonderful it is to be free.
> With all my heart I praise Your Name;

Because of your love I'll never be the same.
From glory to glory You're changing me—
How wonderful it is to be free.

Change springs directly from the new birth. At the moment when a person is born of God new life is imparted—the life of God. This takes root and develops as surely as corn sown in good ground. Immediately change begins. The nature of Christ begins to be revealed. The Bible speaks of the old fallen nature as the 'old man' and the new Christ-nature as the 'new man'. Now the impartation of the latter is an act of God but its growth and development are related to human response. If the old man is fed he will grow, if starved he will fade. If the new man is fed on the things of God he too will develop; if starved, he will never dominate as God intends. Thus the first step in change depends on miracle—the miracle of conversion—but the development of character and the continuing change of personality are not automatically done by God without reference to human willingness and response. We have a part to play.

So we return to our question. 'How do I change? How does it happen? How do I as a born-again believer, having experienced the first God-given change, go on to become like Christ? I know I will need God's constant help but is there a part for me to play?' Basically there are two ways. First, the person who takes Christ as Saviour must also take Him as Lord. (Otherwise I would have grave doubts as to the reality of his salvation.) This means that he comes under the rule of Christ. He comes under discipline—rule, authority—not the rule or authority of a man, but the authority of God. You say, 'Yes, I understand that, but it is still theoretical. What do I actually do? Does it mean that I read the Bible and pray and try to do my best? You see I have tried that but I am not sure that I am much changed.' Yes, you should do all these things but I personally found that these things tended to be vague in my own life and I needed as it were a sharp edge to be introduced to the situation. Many years ago there was a book much in vogue, 'What would Jesus do?' This I found very helpful and I began to put the question to myself consistently, 'What would Jesus do in my place, in my circumstances? What would He have me do?' As problem followed problem and I applied the rule consistently, life changed remarkably. It is a practical piece of advice. Any man who follows this will change. Now this is something *you* can do. It needs no miracle. It only needs consistency and faithfulness. For love of Him it can and should be done. You will find habits will change. You are about to criticise someone and suddenly you apply the rule. What would Jesus do? He would not gossip about anyone. He would not speak unkindly. He would not spread criticism. Suddenly you shut your mouth. Someone attacks you harshly. You are angry. You want to strike back. What would Jesus do? What did He do? He, 'when He was reviled, reviled not again.' You take your anger and your hurt to Him and it ebbs away and for His sake you let love for the persecutor flow as He did on the cross: 'Father forgive them. They know not what they do,' and as dying Stephen did: 'Lay not this sin to their charge.'

A business opportunity opens to you but in the proposition there is a shade of dishonesty. What would Jesus do? You know and He knows. You put the temptation away and walk the road of honesty and obedience.

You are in company. Stories are being told, humorous stories, but not quite reverent, not quite clean. What do you do? Smile to save embarrassment or turn your eyes with a look of holiness that acutely embarrasses the story teller? Do you follow Him faithfully all the way?

The office is having a party. Do you go? 'Well,' you say, 'He took part in social activity in His day. He went to the wedding in Cana of Galilee and Paul said, "If one of them that believe not biddeth you to a feast, and ye are disposed to go; whatsoever is set before you, eat, asking no question for conscience sake" (with reference to the eating of meats). So I am free to go.' What do you do when you get there? At one time you might have suffered little harm but increasingly of late years conduct at many office parties has deteriorated and when you face the question honestly, 'What would Jesus do?' you are compelled to admit He would not take part in unseemly behaviour, in doubtful activity. The drunkenness and uncleanness that characterise so many of those social events are totally alien to Christ. At the end you are compelled to acknowledge that He would take no part in much of the activity and in some cases He would not attend at all. So should it be with you.

The office is having a raffle. You object to gambling on principle but it will seem awfully mean and narrow-minded not to take a ticket. They'll all talk about you and it will be quite embarrassing. Why not just take one and hope it won't come up for then your Christian friends might discover what you had done and you would be embarrassed for another reason? Do you, Daniel-like, take your stand? Christ would never deviate by a hair-breadth from the true course for fear or favour of men. Again apply the rule, 'What would He do?' and the path will be as a shining light before your feet and if the purpose of the raffle is worthy why not give a donation but refuse the ticket saying, 'I do not gamble'?

A friendship has come into your life. You have fallen in love. 'What shall I do? I cannot envisage Christ in such a situation and yet marriage is obviously approved by God. What should I do?' Vary the question. Change it from 'What would Jesus do?' to 'What would Jesus have me do?' and wait for the answer. Guidance, if you are sincere, will surely come. Take it! Do not go by your own natural desire or inclination. Wait for His word.

The areas into which we might go are endless; the rule applies to every walk of life. It should be applied to career, friendships, service for God from fine detail about daily living to the dominating drives and purposes of life. What would Jesus do? You will find that an honest response to this will change you radically—not just change the things you do but the you who do the things.

There is a second area where things need change but *cannot* be changed in this manner. You meet defeat and you meet it again and again until you become hopeless. A few hours before writing this part of this chapter I was speaking to a lady who has come to a stage in her spiritual experience where she is afraid of being quite unable to attain the standard she knows God is demanding. Basically she fears that she will not be able to do it. (Now of course that is in itself a contradiction in terms since if God is demanding something it can be done. He never expects or asks the impossible.) At a deeper level she is failing to believe that God can do the thing in her. Here is the secret. There are things we can do for ourselves and God expects us to do them—but there are other things we cannot do. We come to the end of our tether and in desperation call out to God. It is a good thing to come to this point. We realise our own weakness, our own inadequacy and we are compelled to cast ourselves on Him. It is just at this point that God meets us. Again and again I have seen him perform miracle right here. Again within about 24 hours of writing I listened to a brother testify that after a miraculous conversion and total deliverance from alcohol, he was completely defeated over tobacco. He ultimately cried in desperation to God and was delivered in a moment of time. Again within the same 24-hour period I was called to minister to a lady who could not find freedom herself. About a fortnight earlier a friend of hers had phoned me to speak of this deep need. The first lady knew Christ and had been baptized in the Spirit but had come to a point where sins earlier indulged in were having their repercussions. She had been involved in the occult. The ouija board had featured in her former practices and now she was haunted by horrible nightmares. Her room was invaded from time to time with evil presence. At times the horror of hell was upon her. Yet she loved Christ and strove to serve Him. Her friend, I presume, had knowledge of the ministry of exorcism and brought her to one of our services, at the close of which she sought help. I asked her to go out in the Spirit as far as she could go and at that point open herself fully to God. I realised that she would be afraid but that it was at such a point that evil entities in the body normally manifest themselves. She told me later that she had instinctively known that she could go out in the Spirit to a certain point but that trouble lay beyond that point. This was a clean person, one who hated the darkness she had once been in, and who had renounced the evil practices utterly. Almost as soon as hands were laid on her she reached the critical point and then the foul entity, or entities, came screaming out—as in Scripture crying with a loud voice—in this case the voice was prolonged and there was a sense of rending as they came. She was delivered and peace followed pain. She felt a glorious feeling of space inside her—something had been cleansed away. Christ was very powerful in the operation. With a strong hand He drove the enemy out. Joy and glory followed.

Now that lady needed a miracle. For the second type of change miracle is always necessary. In my own experience there were two occasions which come to mind. In early days I was totally defeated on one issue but in desperation called to God. I had come to the point when I knew my habit was stronger than my power to break it. Previously I had thought in my pride that I could control it. I had to come to the end of myself—to the end of my pride—and acknowledge that not only was I a sinner, but I was a defeated sinner. I could not get out of the pit. In the moment I cast myself on Christ I was delivered. That was a solemn night in my life. I distinctly remember the feeling that if I did not get victory that night I would eventually be a lost soul. It was a life-changing experience and the broken habit never controlled me again.

The second occasion arose in mature years. Something had insidiously got a grip on my life and I came to a point when I realised the thing was wrong. I tried to do something about it but dismally failed. I could put it away in prayer but when I rose from my knees it was there just as strongly as ever. I felt I could go through the motions again and again but it did not make a whit of difference. I was ensnared and I could not get out. There came a moment of severe conviction from God. I knew the thing was sin in His sight and I was desperate. I realised that although one part of me wanted to be free another part was bound beyond my own power to escape—one part did not really want freedom but loved the condition. I cried to God. I was honest and knew that I was not really prepared to do His will but I said in desperation that while I was not willing I was prepared to be made willing and He worked a miracle in a moment of time. The bondage broke and never returned. What had seemed an impossible mountain that I could not get over became in the afterward an insignificant molehill and I gazed in wonder that there should ever have been such difficulty. He had set me free.

How can I be changed? In two ways—by disciplined living in the areas where you can yourself bring the changes—by the action of God in the areas which are beyond your control. In short, by *discipline* and by *miracle*. We are responsible to be free souls by one or other of these two ways. He can change us. He wants to change us and if we are not changed the responsibility is entirely our own. May God bless you all, as you change from glory to glory as you behold His face.

Apart from your own good, will you not come this way, the way of change, for His sake—for love of Him? In all the twelve areas which we have studied and in many more let Him transform us until we show forth the wondrous qualities of the Christ Himself, changed 'from glory to glory as we behold His face.' May we all 'put on Christ' as we behold His qualities.

8

Practising His Presence

In addition to the two main ways in which I indicate
change taking place there are a further two which may be
regarded as akin to the first. If a person disciplines himself
in the following ways changes are likely to be marked.
Thought should be focused on God, and at first the mind
is likely to wander and must be brought back again and
again. If this is persisted in, normally in less than three
days a new habit will have formed and when the mind is
free of normal engagements it will automatically swing
back to God and the things of God. Thus a man may fulfil
Paul's injunction 'to pray without ceasing'. The spirit
dwells in God and human affairs begin to be dealt with at
the circumference of the mind rather than with the whole
of it. That does not mean that they are any less efficiently
dealt with—rather the reverse—but it does mean that
deep and permanent communion with God becomes the
way of life and unspoken prayer can go on at a level deeper
than the mental.

There is nothing supernatural or mystical required to
achieve this position. It is a perfectly natural outcome of
the disciplining of the mind. By determined and consistent

action a new habit is formed and a new pattern established. The whole being, instead of swinging indiscriminately from one interest to another, somewhat like a rudderless ship, is now centred in God Who is the true home of the soul.

A second matter which often requires this same kind of self-discipline is related to our love for Christ. This does not always spring spontaneously in the heart of the believer. I have noticed that many seek counsel in this area, confessing that they do not love God although they deeply desire to. Again and again I have noted that they have frequently suffered from loveless childhoods. Sometimes they have come from broken homes—in most cases something has been lacking in their relationship with one or other or both of their parents. They may say they never felt loved; they were never cuddled as children; they don't know how to love. This is much more widespread than most people imagine.

In my earlier inexperienced days, in dealing with a person who did not love Christ I have known me say, 'Think of how you loved your own father,' only to see the look of pain in the eyes. I learned quickly. The tragedy is that a child *ought* to have parents who love him and are loved by him. They should so represent God to him, that when he comes to an age of responsibility and finds God there should be an easy and instinctive transfer of love and trust to the Heavenly Father—having learned of Him in practical experience through the earthly father. Sadly it is not always so and the deprived person has to start from the beginning.

My counsel is simple and easily followed. If you want love to develop you do not concentrate on love but on the object loved. So with hatred. It grows with concentration on the object or situation hated. If either love or hatred becomes the focus of attention, the emotion inevitably fades. If the cause of either is the focus, the emotion will intensify. Thus if a person wants to love Christ he should not concentrate on the degree to which he does love Him, nor on the measure by which he is lacking in love. He should escape from this profitless activity and turn his attention directly on to Christ Himself. Millions of people have found that to know Christ is to love Him.

In my own experience I found that in my unconverted days, much as I wanted to know and love Christ I was unable to do either. Indeed when I was honest with myself I had to confess, with silent shame, that I did not love Christ at all. I did not even like Him. I respected Him. I wanted to love Him—but there was something about Him which made me intensely uncomfortable. One part of me did not really want Him anywhere near me. The days passed, I found Him as Saviour and in dark hours He came very close and I actually felt His care and His love as a living force and my own love welled up spontaneously in return.

Again when I was baptised in the Spirit I felt a power of love for God quicken within me. I quickly learned that there was a depth of relationship with Christ, a realm of love for and from Christ of which I had not even previously dreamed. He appeared to me as a very lovely and lovable person. The revelation was new and quite unexpected. But all believers do not share this kind of experience. There are other patterns and the testimonies of many love-starved people are remarkably different. They do not seem to be open to love and cataclysmic experiences do not always come upon them. It may be that where pain drove me to Christ and I experienced His love, it can drive some into themselves and into bitterness where they form a shell against emotion, including His love.

So how to get them out into sunshine where His love is all around? I have said, 'To know Him is to love Him' but how are they to get to know Him? This, at one level, needs no miracle. It only needs a very gentle discipline. I counsel such people to set aside fifteen minutes a day—not an hour, not even half an hour—but initially fifteen minutes. I tell them to start by reading part of a Gospel to bring Christ to the forefront of their minds, then to shut the Bible and shut their eyes and envisage Christ, Himself, to meditate on Him, to see Him in action or hear His teaching, as in the reading. Quickly day by day they will get to know Him and a third portion of their fifteen minutes should be devoted to letting themselves positively go out in love to Him. Very soon He will mean more to them than 'all the earth beside'. Let me say it again, 'To know Him is to love Him.'

By these two devices (and again I draw your attention to the fact that they are not supernatural matters), or perhaps I should say methods of discipline, you will find that change in your life will be deep and permanent—and surprisingly fast.

PART 2

A TRANSFORMED LIFE

(Jennifer Jack's Story)

9

Early Days

From as early as I can remember, church and God were part of my life. My parents were committed Christians and belonged to a church which was strongly evangelical; they were keen to have me know God too and so I attended Sunday School, children's services and adult services where I heard the gospel very clearly preached. I knew that the Bible taught that each person had to come as an individual to God, acknowledging a need of a Saviour and asking Christ into the life as Lord. As a child I used to feel guilty each time I heard the gospel and uneasy because I hadn't made any personal response even although I totally believed the truth of what I heard.

Then at a children's campaign where many children were responding, it became a much easier thing to do. I put up my hand in a meeting and waited behind to be counselled. I felt so relieved when I had done this! I didn't need to feel awkward ever again in a gospel service! I had done what was required—I had gone forward at the appeal and I truly believed the doctrine I had heard.

But, unfortunately, nothing had happened inside me. I don't blame the preacher or the campaign—the problem

was in me. I had no real awareness that Jesus Christ
wanted to come right into my life and change me. What
happened was at a mental level only, because I wasn't
looking for anything more, or aware that anything more
was required.

Life continued and I was involved in many church
activities. The church was one which had known revival
and something of that quality was, I believe, still in the
atmosphere. Without understanding this, I just had a
sense that it was good to be there. It was warm and secure.
Then, when I was fourteen, there came a major change. A
young couple in the church were keen to see younger
people find Christ deeply. They themselves were baptised
in the Spirit (the church was Pentecostal) and they knew
that others needed this experience. They arranged for a
busload of us to go to a Pentecostal Holiday Centre in
Wales for two weeks holiday and, unknown to us, they
made sure that the invited speaker for one of the weeks
was a man whom God was using to bring people into the
experience of the Baptism in the Spirit. At that time this
ministry was much less widespread than it is today and the
man concerned, Mr George Deakin, was used deeply in it
(and still is).[1] We arrived at the Holiday Centre and the
holiday took its course with meetings interspersed with
other activities. Then on the Thursday, a 'tarry meeting'
was arranged to run between five and seven in the evening,
before dinner. I listened to the announcement with no
particular interest. I had heard of such meetings (as I said,
our church was Pentecostal) but they were in no way
relevant to me. I didn't even consider going. However, the
girl who was responsible for our group being there was
going round the bedrooms telling us individually that we
really should go. It was, she said, a tremendous opportunity to receive an experience which would change our
lives. I listened politely but I still wasn't interested. But I
gradually realised that almost everyone else had decided to

go. Indeed, all the others in my room—six of them—were going. I was horrified. I didn't want to go, but neither did I want to miss out on something that they were all going to be part of! When I turned my mind to consider going, I realised that I was really quite frightened. I knew that people who were baptised in the Spirit 'spoke in tongues' and this brought me face to face with an experience which was obviously supernatural and therefore disturbing. I didn't know what to do. Eventually, I let the others talk me into going to the meeting, mainly because I didn't want to be left out. Hardly a very worthy motive for seeking the Baptism!

At five o'clock we gathered in the meeting tent beside the building where we were staying and we were seated on three sides of a square, around a wooden platform at the front. Mr Deakin talked to us very simply for a short time and I can still remember what he said. He spoke of the fact that the Holy Spirit was poured out on the early Church on the Day of Pentecost and that this happened after Jesus had been glorified (when He ascended into Heaven). He said that the same principle still applied—when Jesus is glorified, the Spirit is poured out. He asked us not to think about the Baptism we were seeking, not to think about speaking in tongues, but simply to glorify Jesus—something we could all do. We could praise Him and thank Him for dying on the cross, for saving us, for every good thing which He had done for us.

The speaking lasted for only a few minutes and I had listened very carefully. We turned to prayer and I tried very hard to do just as he said. I suppose I was tense and nervous; I was certainly unused to praying for anything longer than a few minutes. After a short time I became aware that something was happening at the opposite side of the square from where I was sitting. Someone was being baptised in the Spirit. It was a boy whom I knew—one of my friends—just an ordinary teenager like me and something tremendous was happening to him. As the Holy

Spirit fell, he was being baptised, but instead of *speaking* in tongues, as most people do, he was *singing* in tongues. This really made me sit up! It was obvious that God was doing something wonderful. No way was this the boy I knew—he was in touch with another power and something very lovely was happening to him. Suddenly God was very close.

I turned back to prayer and, for what was the first time in my life, I began to pray in earnest. I really wanted *this* God to come to me. I remembered what I'd been told— glorify Jesus. I prayed, thanking Jesus for going to the cross for me, and at first as I pictured three crosses on a hill while I prayed, everything seemed very dark and prayer was hard. However, I persisted—I was determined to find whatever that boy had found, and after a time it was as if there was a light on the cross as I prayed and tried to reach God. Hope was born in me, Calvary seemed much more real and Jesus was much nearer. I felt drawn to the cross and very close to the warm Presence of Christ. In a small way, it was rather like the experience the disciples had on the Mount of Transfiguration. At first they were focusing on so many aspects of that wonderful scene, but then their attention was directed to Jesus alone, and His glory and His true identity were revealed to them in a special way. My experience was at a much more basic level, but as I prayed, all the other facets of the scene at the cross seemed to fade away as Jesus drew near and He became a real, living Person Who was offering salvation to me, as an individual. I honestly believe that in that moment I found salvation.

Time passed and eventually one or two people came to pray with me for the Baptism—I was fairly near the end of the row and I discovered later that many others had by this time been baptised. As we prayed, one word from another language seemed to come to mind but I was afraid that I might be making it up myself or subconsciously copying others around me. However, after a few moments I was so desperate not to miss out on what God had for me that I decided to speak the word I had, trusting that those ministering to me would stop me and correct me if I was doing something wrong. At first I was hesitant and doubtful, one part of me analysing what I was saying and the other wanting to enter into the experience, but after a few minutes an assurance seemed to come and I stopped thinking about the words and simply allowed a lovely well of praise and warmth to bubble up from inside me and pour out to God. The tongues were flowing freely (as I was told afterwards by others) but I wasn't thinking of what I was saying—I was simply glorifying Jesus and the Spirit was falling.

That meeting finished shortly after seven o'clock. We were all late for dinner, and yet it felt as if we had been there for only a few minutes. The experience I had that day made God very real and in the weeks that followed life was very bright—in fact, the world seemed to be literally brighter and there was a real joy and cleanness inside.

Note

[1] Since the time of writing, Mr Deakin has passed away.

10

Fading Glory

When we returned home things went well for a time but, in me at least, there came a fading of the experience which had been so bright. Then, about six months later I made a wrong decision which was to prove disastrous in my spiritual life. Often we think that fourteen year olds are not terribly aware of spiritual rights and wrongs and as a result we expect little of them. I think this is very far from the truth. I knew very clearly at that age that a particular road was wrong but I gradually talked myself into going that way, convincing myself that it was perfectly all right. Because of one deliberate wrong choice I found myself caught up in a whole situation where my thoughts and my heart very quickly and very deeply began to move along a different pathway from the one which had led me to God. The love of the heart was certainly not Christ and my life became centred on other things.

During this time, things on the outside might have appeared very good. I attended church very regularly—several times a week—and, indeed, kept a very high moral standard in my life. I helped to run Scripture Union meetings as a senior pupil in school. But my heart was in other things and other relationships. Oddly enough, all the time I knew that I was trying to go in two quite different directions and that a decision would have to be made at some point—one way or the other. And the strange thing was that I knew I could never turn my back totally on God. I knew He was real. But none of this helped me to make the break that was required. My heart was entangled in a completely different way of life and it seemed too costly to change.

Things continued in this way until I left school. At that point a great emptiness came into my life. Most of my friends were waiting to enjoy the student world but, instinctively, I knew that to go their way would be to cross a forbidden line. The school social scene was one thing, the university one was quite another. I went to university and for most of my first year was very unhappy. I had no friends following the same course as myself—in fact, no close friends at the same university—and my best friends were thoroughly immersed in a way of life that I felt was closed to me. One particular relationship had come to an end and on top of all this I was a very diffident person and had no confidence that I would cope with university exams.

11

A Deeper Call

I did join the Christian Union, where several people were very friendly, but somehow I didn't relax and didn't feel at home. Then, in conversation with one of the C.U. girls, I discovered that she, like myself, attended a Pentecostal church. She told me that a small group of students who were baptised in the Spirit met on a Friday evening for a prayer meeting and she asked if I would like to come. I wasn't at all keen! I didn't go to 'prayer meetings' and I wondered if these people would pray very intellectual and learned prayers which I could never emulate. I made excuses, but every time we met the invitation was repeated and the girl so genuinely wanted me to come that it became embarrassing to go on refusing and I eventually agreed. The following Friday we met and walked to the flat where the meeting was held. All my preconceptions about the meeting were shattered. It was no 'intellectual' gathering but a meeting of people who in a very simple and sincere way were seeking for God—and finding Him. I can't now remember the order of things, but at some point we turned to prayer and immediately as people began to speak quietly in tongues I sensed the same atmosphere as I had felt at my Baptism, almost four years earlier. God was very kind to me and, as I was prayed with, the Holy Spirit came and I began to speak in tongues, something I had not done since shortly after my Baptism. I felt in that meeting that I had come home. There was a security, a warmth and a love in God's Presence—and a feeling of belonging there. It was lovely.

After that I didn't have to be coaxed. I was at the meeting every week and even kept a contact over the summer holiday period which began several weeks later. When term began again in October, I was back at the meetings but I was now beginning to sense that there was something more. I loved the meeting each Friday, but for the rest of the week my life seemed to be unchanged and I felt that something was wrong in that. My ordinary life was very respectable—but it wasn't spiritual, and I sensed that this wasn't right.

Several weeks later a Conference weekend was organised for the students who were meeting on a Friday and for other people who wished to attend. It was run by Struthers Memorial Church, through whom the student group came into being. Of course, I wanted to go and I took with me a boy from my own church who had just started university. I was really looking forward to the weekend, but this was partly because it was a holiday weekend with new friends and that brought its own kind of excitement. We duly arrived at the Centre and the first meeting took place. It was then that something happened which shocked me into taking spiritual things much more seriously and allowing God to work a fundamental change in my life. The meeting was wonderful—I could sense that—but I was dismayed to find that I was totally unaffected by it.

It was a dreadful experience to sense that God was really there but that I was unmoved and untouched. Then I was told that the boy I had brought—who had been sitting elsewhere in the hall with some boys to whom he'd been introduced—had been wonderfully baptised in the Spirit. One part of me was pleased—after all, that was why he'd been invited!—but another part was very troubled and upset. Here was someone totally new to this kind of meeting and he had found God in a very real way—it was so obvious: he was radiant with happiness. I had known God already—surely I should have been more able to tune to what God was doing than this new lad? Instead I seemed so much less able. Was I so spiritually dead, so out of touch with God that I couldn't be part of a meeting of this kind? I left the hall and went upstairs. I talked to another girl in my room and discovered that she hadn't really felt part of the meeting either. But this didn't help me feel any better! Eventually, I went to bed.

As I lay there, there was real turmoil inside me. Suddenly, I was no longer interested in a holiday weekend, in friends or anything else. Only one thing mattered—that I would be through to God and involved in and part of what was happening in the meetings. It was intolerable to be an outsider, cut off from His Presence and His Love. Priorities all changed as I thought of this and I was prepared to lay aside everything in a single-minded search for God.

When I wakened in the morning I just knew that something was going to happen—in fact, that something had begun happening. There was a real anticipation within me and I was almost trembling. After breakfast, the meeting began and in due course we turned to pray. Very quickly, I became aware that God was very near and what I sensed was the fire of His Holy Spirit. It wasn't a frightening thing but something awesome and full of power. Two things happened simultaneously. As I opened myself to find God and the very deepest part of me reached out for Him, that fire came sweeping in and it burnt and destroyed so much of the rubbish that had been filling up my life. It was like a huge lump of 'self' being taken and burnt in a few moments of time. Selfishness and self-

centredness came under its blaze. Secondly, and at exactly
the same time, that fire was kindling a love for Jesus
Christ—something that was so strong that it was almost
tangible and so powerful that it caused me to tremble.
Deeps in my personality, which were unknown to me,
were opened up that day, and opened up to God. It was as
if a whole new dimension of life was opened and I realised
that fundamentally we are spiritual creatures, not earthly
ones. There is a depth and a fulfilment in the spiritual
dimension which is of a glorious and eternal kind.

The rest of the Conference all merged into one for me.
That night I hardly slept because I felt more wonderfully
awake and alive than I ever had before. Each meeting was
a coming in to that same glorious fire and between meetings the warmth and the wonder of it were still there. It
was impossible to think of anything else. It reminds me of
the verse of Scripture: 'The Lord Whom ye seek shall
suddenly come to His temple.' Christ had come and it was
truly wonderful. He can do so much so quickly and in that
one experience my life was changed more than I can ever
describe. There was only one life and that was Christ.

I was asked to testify to what had happened, in one of
the Conference meetings. I don't think I made a very good
job of it because I was still so emotionally moved and the
experience was so new. But as I spoke I did sense that the
Spirit was somehow transmitting the essence of my experience, despite my own inadequacies. Spiritual fire spreads
just as natural fire does and I quickly found that all I
wanted to do was to keep the fire burning and to allow it to
spread as widely and as quickly as possible.

12

The Fire Burns

I returned home on the Sunday night and within an hour I
happened to meet one of my friends from the church I
attended. Immediately there was an opening to tell her
about my weekend and I could see the hunger and interest
in her as I spoke. I could sense that the fire was spreading.
I didn't feel that I was doing anything at all. I was carrying
something from God and it was spreading to souls whom
He wanted to reach. The next Friday she came to the
meeting and God met her. Others followed and over a
period of time about thirty came. Some were baptised in
the Spirit; others received a fresh infilling.

As a result of this influx of people, the meetings had to
move to a public hall in Partick (Glasgow) and were advertised. There began a period of about eighteen months
when not one Friday passed without someone being baptised in the Spirit. That fire was burning in those meetings
(in other lives as well as my own) and it was glorious to be
there.

It was, in fact, out of these meetings that two churches
were born—the Glasgow and Falkirk branches of
Struthers Church—and that same fire burns right at the

heart of the works. (I must make it clear that I am not attributing the growth of the work and the founding of the churches to what happened in my life alone. My experience was part of a much wider moving of the Spirit and other lives were as deeply and more deeply involved. But this account is a personal testimony and so it focuses on what happened in one life and how this related to the work of God as a whole.)

Out of the Partick meetings, the Glasgow branch of the Church evolved and I was called to assist Miss Mary Black in the leadership. A public role of this kind was not something I coveted but it was very clear that it was God-given and so there was no argument on my part. (I had, some time before this, had a long controversy with God over the issue of taking part in public prayer. God was asking me to do it and I found it almost an impossibility to obey. And so I argued that it wasn't necessary for me to pray. I was involved in the meetings in other ways, particularly in personal ministry to others, and I was keen to see God move. But my refusal brought a barrier between myself and the close place with God which I had known. After a long struggle I came back to the place where God could have everything—and that included public prayer, if He asked me to do this. Through that experience I learned a valuable lesson—never to argue when God asks for anything. And I have never done so again. It may have taken me time to yield an issue fully but I have always co-operated with God and asked for His help to do what was required. At first I couldn't understand why public prayer was so important but I now feel that I can see something of its significance. In anointed prayer a person becomes a vehicle for the Holy Spirit and in doing this learns to come under His control when speaking. This is extremely important and is a stepping stone to inspired preaching and prophecy. And so when I was put into a public role in the Glasgow church, I didn't argue, although I did not find it easy.)

Later, a small group from Falkirk started attending the Glasgow meetings regularly and transport soon became a problem. It became clear that it was necessary to hold some kind of gathering in Falkirk and a house group was started. It was with a feeling of horror that I learned that I was to be in charge, but there was a clear knowledge that God was in it and so there was no argument. It is now a good number of years since the Falkirk meetings began. Soon we had a full range of services and we met in public halls of various sizes and descriptions. Gradually growth came, mainly through the addition of young people, exactly in accordance with a vision which had been given earlier relative to the work as a whole. As things began to take root and there came a sense of expansion and new horizons I longed for a building of our own, but despite efforts on our part to secure a site on which to build or a building to convert for our own use, no progress was made. On one occasion in particular, we held a prayer meeting to pray about the issue. God was very strongly present and there was a sense that we had an access to Heaven on the matter. There was a feeling that God had the situation in His Hand and further prayer was not necessary. I remember, very clearly, that at the end of the meeting I opened my Bible and God gave two clear verses from the book of Jeremiah, one of which was: 'Yea, I will rejoice over them to do them good, and I will plant them in this land assuredly with my whole heart and with my whole soul' (Jer 32:41).

There was reassurance in the verses given and a sense that it would all be worked out in God's time.

Then about three years ago, word came to us that an extremely suitable building was coming on to the market—the old Town Mission. It was ideal in so many ways—very near the town centre, car-parking adjacent to the building, the size and shape just right so that a small number did not look ridiculous but there was still room for considerable expansion. It was so much more suitable than anything we had looked at before. From the moment we heard of the building, it seemed just right and before very long it was ours and work began on its refurbishment. The building was in need of substantial renovation and a tremendous amount of voluntary labour was put in. When we officially 're-opened' it in December, 1986 the place had been transformed. In the building there is a lovely sense of the Presence of God—it is a place where God has moved deeply on many occasions over the years—and we anticipate that in days to come this will greatly increase.

But while the acquisition of a building is important, it is very secondary to the spiritual building of the church and over the years God has made it very clear that it is no light work that He wants in any life. Again and again His Holy Spirit has come amongst us to save souls, to baptise in the Holy Spirit, and to change people, meeting needs of every kind. The depth of change in some lives has been remarkable and at the time of writing there is a sense of a growing number who are beginning to know the strength and the freedom that there is in Christ and who are learning to come into the spiritual dimension where He wants them to live.

13

Paths of Pain

I suppose it is true that almost every life has its share of suffering and Christians are certainly not exempt. From childhood, my own attitude has always been that Christianity does not bring freedom from suffering and pain (as many would suggest) but rather that it provides an inner strength to enable the individual to cope and to overcome when circumstances are difficult.

I was brought up with suffering very close to me. When I was a baby of six months, my mother became ill with rheumatoid arthritis and within six short months she was so crippled that it was difficult for her to walk. At three points in the years that followed, she spent six-month stretches in hospital—when I was three years old and seven years old she was in traction for six-month periods to try to straighten her knee joints which were locking in a bent and twisted position; and when I was eleven years old she was admitted for an operation to remove one knee joint to free her from at least some of the pain and to enable her to stand upright. Pain was part of everyday life for her and yet many people frequently remarked on her cheerfulness and strong spirit. Our home was certainly not a depressing place; my memories are of a very happy and secure childhood. I think I was shielded to some extent, quite deliberately, by my parents, but the happiness and security were certainly not artificial. God was at the centre of life as far as they were concerned and He was in control. From there came strength, and life went on.

Then when I was in my twenties there came the shattering news that my father had cancer and had only weeks to live. I was totally unprepared for this although he himself had known instinctively that his illness (undiagnosed at that time) was terminal and had taken steps to set all his business in order in a final way before entering hospital. We had only a few weeks to prepare ourselves before he died.

When it came near the time of his dying, God was very, very close. As we gathered around that hospital bed and watched him go, all I could feel was an exultant joy. Many people will not understand this. Later there were tears and grief—he was deeply missed and mourned—but at the moment of his passing it was as if I shared in a small way something of what he had entered into. Heaven came very near and it was impossible in these moments to be sad or even to want him back—it would have been so selfish, because where he had gone was so much better.

I was, of course, concerned about my mother. Her needs and her suffering would in many ways be so much greater than mine. I knew that my dad had always voiced his hope that my mother would die first so that she wouldn't be left to cope with her illness and disablement without his support. But there was no need for worry. A conversation she had, in my presence, with one of her friends put it so clearly. She said, 'I never dreamed I could feel like this. There's no fear, no worry. There's such a sense of peace.'

In an unusual way God had prepared me, some months earlier, for moving from the place where I worked and after my father died I was able to work near my home. My mother needed help and I was able to be home at lunchtimes and by four o'clock in the afternoon. We had also moved house shortly before my father's death to an area where it was much more convenient to use a wheel-chair and these changes all helped to make life much easier. These and other circumstances were evidence of the loving provision of a God Who cared.

Things continued in this way for a few years and then God gave clear warning of a coming change. In a meeting one evening, for no particular reason I felt a very real weight of unhappiness come on me. I was puzzled because there was nothing to which I could relate it. But as I began to analyse why I felt this way, I knew it related to my mother. At that time there was no sign at all of any change in her condition which had been static for many years. The pain had receded to a great extent but the crippling was severe. After the service, I spoke to someone about what I had felt, indicating that I did not really understand the reason for it.

In the weeks that followed I watched my mother's con-dition very carefully and within a few months I began to detect a change. She was less able to manage on her own for any length of time. What mobility she had began to go—not because of the arthritis but because she seemed to be very sluggish in her movements (she was only a little over 60 years old). I made arrangements for her to have almost constant care while I was at work and then things deteriorated even further as cerebral spasms occurred. I left work to nurse her. Her condition was very unusual and demanded very specialised nursing care which only my father and I had known how to provide. It wasn't skill that was required, but knowledge of the patient and we could spare her intense suffering simply because we knew how to move her from one position to another.

She then went into a period of steady decline until her death, eighteen months later. At first, my job was held open for me but after some months it was impossible for this to continue and so I resigned. I knew that she would not recover and that I would be needed until her life ended. This, I must stress, was no sacrifice. It would have been far more difficult to leave her or see her hospitalised where she would have suffered so much that I could have spared her. Over these months I was shut in, sometimes for weeks and months without being out of the house at all. I had very real support from friends—mostly Christian friends who knew God and who visited regularly. This brought a real strengthening; but there was also a strong sense of God's presence which filled the house. Again, there was a security and a peace. There was no worry about the future—about the approaching death or about my own future—just a sense that everything was in God's hands and it was absolutely safe there. During this time I was ill myself with sciatica and shingles but again God provided and with support from friends I was able to continue nursing my mother.

One morning I sensed a significant change in her condition and when the doctor was called he told me what I already knew. She was dying and would last only a few hours. When the moment came, there was just a sense of her spirit entering into the peace and the love of God. It was very different from my father's death but no less wonderful. The room was filled with the gentleness of Christ and there was a sense of a struggle being ended. For many days afterwards I was conscious of her being so much more alive than she had ever been—completely whole and well.

And what of my own position afterwards? Within days I had assurance of a job. The position I had held before had been a promoted one and I was back at work for only three weeks when that same position was advertised. Had I not been in the Authority's employment by that time I would not have been eligible to apply. As it was, I applied and was re-appointed to my own post. God took care of even that.

At home there was, for a time, a feeling of loneliness. Because of her illness my mother had always been at home. Never had I come in to an empty house. And she was a particularly cheerful, outgoing person who always wanted to hear about our day at work or wherever else we had been. A silent house was difficult to adjust to. But two things helped. Firstly, over the time of her final illness her speech and her brain were affected and so I was able to adjust gradually to losing her as a companion and friend. Secondly, Mr Black said something to me which helped a great deal. 'See your home as a base from which to work for God. Your work is out there, in the world and in the Church—home is a place from which to operate.' These words helped tremendously in the period of adjustment.

I do not want to leave the impression that the Christian life is one of hardship. But suffering and distress are undoubtedly part of the human condition and I have found again and again that God is there to meet me in difficult times and He brings with Him a strength and peace which not only help me cope but cause me to emerge as a more complete person and with a stronger faith in and knowledge of Himself.

God is greater than any circumstance and I am becoming increasingly aware that there is a place in Him where we can rise above every situation and where we can also come to know the abundance of His Life and Power.

14

Author's Reflections and Observations

I first met Miss Jack when she was about eighteen and was quickly impressed by her honesty and integrity. She had just commenced university and soon became friendly with two of my daughters who were there at the same time. I was a witness to some of the early spiritual experiences which she has herself described and was particularly impressed by the coming of very real fire upon her life and some of the consequences which flowed from this. She immediately began to bring people to the Glasgow meetings where many were baptised in the Spirit. She had a share in the growth of the gathering which soon could not be housed in a flat, but had to go into a public hall until a permanent building was obtained.

It is at my request that she has written the chapter 'Paths of Pain'; and again I witnessed at first hand most of the things she has described. A particularly quiet and unassuming person, Jennifer will probably be highly embarrassed to see this testimony in print. Hers is a life which speaks very sweetly of Christ. She puts Him first in her living. On the public side she is a first-rate preacher and is used in bringing others into the Baptism in the

Spirit. In recent years, after a time of particular purging, she has been used in the deliverance ministry.

Most people have particular qualities which are distinctive. In Jennifer's case three things come particularly to mind. I was reminded of the first as I read her testimony. She is a highly efficient person, an excellent organiser, and this has been appreciated in secular as well as in church circles. All of this kind of thing she omits to mention. Self-effacement is one of her most noticeable characteristics.

The second quality, if I may call it a quality, is quite unique. I suppose all spiritual people do have things which are unique to themselves. In Jennifer's case I became aware at a very early stage that as she ministered under the power of the Holy Spirit there came through her a peculiarly lovely emanation of Christ. It is quite distinctive and is almost like a fragrance. Many have benefited from the sweetness of her ministry and she has been used both in public preaching and in dealing with people individually, the latter frequently by the laying on of hands.

The third distinctive characteristic relates to her preaching. It is at times unusually original. She is able to get inside a story and present insights which to me, at least, can be quite new. It is a valuable gift.

The fire which came into her life to which she has herself referred was also quite distinctive. I remember its coming clearly. It transformed her life and was indeed a felt thing and many were affected by it. I often ask her to speak on this subject for the sake of others. People frequently fail to realise the potential which lies in the Baptism in the Spirit. They regard it as an 'end' experience rather than a 'beginning'. If it is regarded as an apex rather than an entrance into an ever-deepening life in God the person concerned is apt to fall back to a comparatively low level. I often think that people come to Christ and reach a high point. Frequently they fall back to a position not far above the level from which they rose. Certainly they have changed their social grouping but apart from that there may be little to distinguish them, at least outwardly, from the world in general. What has gone wrong? If there has been genuine conversion the soul must, in that glorious moment, have been in touch with God and God delights to communicate with His child. Too frequently direct dealing with God fails to continue. Fellow Christians heap the young believer with advice, usually well-meaning, but often providing little more than a code of practice—a list of instructions—do's and don'ts—and before he knows it he has stopped listening both to, and for, the direct voice of God. His Christianity has become largely second-hand.

Time passes and he hears that others are receiving great blessing. They are being baptised in the Spirit. He is interested and envious. In due time he too receives. It is a wonderful hour. He reaches a new high. He is 'Pentecostal' now. Things will never be the same again! All too often this is just not true. From the hour of his conversion he should have depended on God's guidance. Human guidance was substituted, with resulting failure. God is now in control in the hour of the Baptism. What happens? All too often the process is repeated. Men give advice and often the person is scarcely off his knees before he is himself again in control. Having been *under* the power of the Spirit he should remain under the Spirit for the rest of a lifetime. But no! He gets up and takes charge. Instead of *being used* by the power he decides *to use* the power and work for God.

In the case of my own Baptism I was literally hardly off my knees before someone told me that after he was baptised he walked on air for about three weeks—but he said, 'You'll come down, you know.' There was I, newly born so far as this experience was concerned, on a height with God—and almost the first thing I heard was a respected Pentecostal gentleman telling me that my feet would come down again. I said never a word but I resolved inside myself that by God's grace my feet would never come down. My 'Pentecost' was dearly bought and greatly valued and I was not relinquishing one jot or tittle. From time to time through the years my feet *have* come down, but I have never accepted the 'down' position as normal or the will of God; and one good thing I learned about the 'down' position is that it can be like the bottom of a pool— a good place from which to kick upwards if one is drowning as I once was. From the bottom you can take a mighty leap to break surface and shout for help. God is there to give just that. The 'up' position is His will for His people. Have you never noticed that the New Testament says remarkably little about revival—simply because the *living* condition should be *normal* for the Church?—there should be no 're-' about it; the Bible neither envisages the Christian living at a low level nor does it legislate for it, as a normal way of life.

In Pentecostal circles we have too often forgotten the word of John the Baptist, 'There cometh One after me the latchet of whose shoes I am not fit to unloose. He shall baptize you with the Holy Ghost and fire'—*and fire*. It burns wherever it goes. It cannot be concealed or tamed. It either burns or it goes out. Jennifer had an experience of fire and many have been kindled by the flame. I have found her testimony to her receiving of fire and the effect of it very valuable through the years in instructing others.

I should say a word about family background. Mrs Jack, Jennifer's mother, was quite a remarkable woman. Disabled with arthritis from the time of her daughter's birth, she experienced times of excruciating pain, yet never once through the years of my being acquainted with her did I ever hear her complain or indulge in self-pity. She was constantly outgoing and caring in her attitude to others. Frequently disappointed through people who taught that she could be healed more or less at any time, she 'endured as seeing Him Who is invisible.' Her suffering never embittered her but rather a sweetness came from her life.

Mr Jack was a godly man and came of a godly home. His mother was a deep woman of prayer who regularly walked long distances to church. He himself was a man of integrity. Much respected in the community, he served God and walked ever closer to Him as his days on earth drew to a close. I had the privilege of being with both Mr and Mrs Jack when they died. In Mrs Jack's case it was like a falling asleep after a long and painful voyage. She had reached a stage where she was exceedingly frail. Her skin was paper-thin and she had to be handled with very great care. One evening she very quietly 'fell asleep' in Christ. It was most peaceful.

In Mr Jack's case, I had a most remarkable experience. He had been ill for a time and during that time I got to know him deeply. He had a great love for God. For many years he had followed Him and perhaps his greatest regret was that he had not done more for Him. I will never forget that deathbed or the moment of his actual passing. I was with Mrs Jack and Jennifer when the moment of his release came. Suddenly I found myself going with him not just to the brink of death but my spirit seemed to go to the very portals of Heaven. I was overcome with the flood of glory into which he went. I spontaneously prophesied. The glory of God surrounded that bed. Neither before nor since have I ever experienced this in the same way although I have been at many deathbeds and know the action of God again and again in such hours. In Mr Jack's case I was reminded of Bunyan's Mr Valiant-for-Truth who, going into the last dark river, said, ' "Death where is thy sting?" and as he went down deeper he said, "Grave where is thy victory?" So he passed over and all the trumpets sounded for him on the other side.'

Jennifer's indeed is a godly heritage!

BOOK ORDERS

The books advertised on the previous pages are being made available to Christian booksellers throughout the country, but if you have any difficulty in obtaining your supply, you may order directly from New Dawn Books, c/o 27 Denholm Street, Greenock, Scotland, PA16 8RH.

········· ORDER FORM ··········

Please send me the books indicated below:

Quantity	Title	Price
	Reflections on the Baptism in the Holy Spirit	£2.25
	Reflections on the Gifts of the Spirit	£2.75
	Reflections on a Song of Love (A commentary on 1 Cor 13)	£1.25
	A Trumpet Call to Women	£2.50
	Consider Him (Twelve Qualities of Christ)	£2.25
	Battle for the Body	£2.95
	The Clash of Tongues with Glimpses of Revival	£2.50

Signature ....

Address ....

....

....

When ordering please send purchase price plus 30p per book to help cover the cost of postage and packaging.